real
meditation
in *minutes* a day

JOSEPH ARPAIA, M.D.
LOBSANG RAPGAY, PH.D.

real
meditation
in *minutes* a day

OPTIMIZING YOUR

PERFORMANCE, RELATIONSHIPS,

SPIRITUALITY, AND HEALTH

WISDOM PUBLICATIONS
BOSTON

Wisdom Publications, Inc.
199 Elm Street
Somerville MA 02144 USA
www.wisdompubs.org

Library of Congress Cataloging-in-Publication Data
Arpaia, Joseph.
 Real meditation in minutes a day : optimizing your performance, relationships, spirituality, and health / Joseph Arpaia, Lobsang Rapgay.
     p. cm.
 Includes bibliographical references and index.
 ISBN 0-86171-556-X (pbk. : alk. paper)
 1. Meditation—Buddhism. I. Lobsang Rapgay. II. Title.
 BQ5612.A77 2008
 294.3'4435—dc22
                                    2008012116
12 11 10 09 08
 5 4 3 2 1

Cover design by Pema Studios. Interior design by Dede Cummings. Set in New Caledonia 11.5/15.5.

Wisdom Publications' books are printed on acid-free paper and meet the guidelines for permanence and durability of the Production Guidelines for Book Longevity of the Council on Library Resources.

Printed in the United States of America.

This book was produced with environmental mindfulness. We have elected to print this title on 30% PCW recycled paper. As a result, we have saved the following resources: 23 trees, 16 million BTUs of energy, 2,053 lbs. of greenhouse gases, 8,524 gallons of water, and 1,095 lbs. of solid waste. For more information, please visit our website, www.wisdompubs.org. This paper is also FSC certified. For more information, please www.fscus.org.

from Joseph Arpaia
I would like to dedicate this work
to my late cousin, Kathy Mazza

from Lobsang Rapgay
I would like to dedicate this work
to the late junior tutor to His Holiness the Dalai Lama,
Kyabje Trijang Dorje Chang (1900–1981),
and my late father Karma Wangchuk
and mother Pasang Lhamu.

contents

PART I
four practices for developing
the five mental qualities

PART II
applying meditation in your daily life

real
meditation
in *minutes* a day

THE DALAI LAMA
foreword

THROUGH MEDITATION, we can train our minds in such a way that their negative qualities are abandoned and their positive qualities are generated and enhanced. In general, we talk about two types of meditation: analytical and single-pointed. First, the object of meditation is put through a process of analysis in which we repeatedly attempt to gain acquaintance with the subject matter. When we have gained confidence about the object of meditation, the mind is made to concentrate on that without further analysis. This combination of analytical and concentrative meditation is an effective technique for properly training our minds.

The importance of this practice arises from the fundamental fact that each and every one of us innately desires happiness and does not want misery. Whether we experience happiness or sorrow in life depends largely on the state of our minds. Furthermore, the way in which the experiences we encounter affect our lives also depends on the mind. When we misuse our mental potential, we make mistakes and suffer unpleasant consequences. On the other hand, when the mind's potential is skillfully harnessed, we derive positive and pleasant results.

The authors of this book, Joseph P. Arpaia and Lobsang Rapgay, have drawn on the Tibetan Buddhist traditions of meditation and on an understanding of Western cognitive psychology to present meditative practice in a way that readers will find is actually effective. I congratulate them for their efforts, and offer my prayers that readers who employ these techniques will indeed be successful in increasing a sense of peace and happiness in their own lives, thereby contributing to greater peace and happiness in the world at large.

His Holiness the Fourteenth Dalai Lama,
Tenzin Gyatso

meditation: what it is, and how this book will teach you to do it

meditate. *verb.* (1) Exercise the mental faculties in thought or contemplation. (2) a. Muse over, reflect; consider; study; ponder. Also, plan by turning over in the mind, conceive mentally. b. Fix one's attention on; observe intently or with interest.

—*Shorter Oxford English Dictionary, Fifth Edition*

MEDITATION is exercise for your mind. Just as exercise for your body improves your physical abilities, meditation will improve your mental abilities. Meditation enhances whatever you do with your mind: it helps you perceive more clearly, it improves your thinking and memory, and it enhances your creativity. You develop your mind into an ever more effective tool for living.

There are many myths about meditation, which can interfere with our ability to use it effectively; so let's make clear what meditation is *not*.

xiii

MEDITATION: THE MYTHS

Myth 1: Meditation is Eastern.

Meditation has been practiced by Christians for almost two thousand years, and Jews, Muslims, and those of other traditions have meditative practices as well. Even if many meditation techniques come from Eastern traditions, there is nothing to prevent others from adopting those techniques to develop their minds.

Myth 2: Meditation is for religious people.

You do not have to be religious to benefit from meditation, just as you do not have to be an athlete in order to benefit from physical exercise. Meditation is exercise for the mind. You can use it for spiritual development. You can also use it to improve your health, your effectiveness at work, and your relationships with others.

Myth 3: Meditation takes hours per day.

If you have hours to spend, then you can certainly spend them meditating. But you don't need hours to benefit from meditating. In fact, even fifteen or twenty minutes per day will help you significantly.

Myth 4: Meditation is relaxation.

Meditation can help you *learn* to relax. However, sometimes you need to feel more energized. There are meditations that can help you speed up when you need to speed up, and meditations that can help you slow down when you need to slow down.

Myth 5: Meditation is stopping thoughts.

Meditation teaches you how to change your usual thoughts so you can think differently, and more effectively. Meditation also develops mental activities such as perceiving or imagining, which are different from thinking.

Myth 6: Meditation is blanking out the mind.

Meditation is training the mind. You meditate in order to develop your mind, not blank it out.

Myth 7: Meditation is used by cults.

Cults use the myth that meditation involves blanking out the mind to disguise brainwashing techniques as meditation. Since meditation strengthens the mind, and the mind's ability to inquire and analyze, meditation is, in fact, a good antidote to cult techniques.

Myth 8: I need a guru or teacher to learn meditation.

A good teacher can and certainly will help. However, one of the most important teachers is your own experience. As you continue to practice, you'll learn to evaluate the effects of the techniques and find those that work best for you.

This book teaches a system of precise meditation instructions that enables you to achieve personal growth and transformation in our fast-paced world. You will be able to maintain all your responsibilities and even feel more on top of them. You will discover how to live amid chaos without becoming chaotic. You will learn to heal faster and work more efficiently. You will also learn to be more peaceful with others, and have a more fulfilling spiritual life.

The book is divided into two parts. In the first part we explain some general principles and teach four basic meditation practices that develop five core mental qualities. In the second part you'll learn how to apply these basic techniques to improve your health, performance, relationships, and spirituality.

WHO IS THIS FOR AND WHAT CAN YOU EXPECT?

We have taught these techniques successfully to young and old, to those with and without advanced degrees, and to people with and without a spiritual background. The only requirement is a willingness to practice the techniques and learn from your experiences.

People who meditate report the following kinds of benefits:

- Reduced stress, even when under pressure
- Improved sleep
- More energy
- Clearer thinking
- Improved memory
- Enhanced creativity
- More peaceful relationships
- A greater sense of meaning
- A deeper experience of spirituality

You will learn about your core mental qualities and how those can be balanced and strengthened. The principles and techniques we will be teaching are common to many traditions.

You do not need to flee to a monastery or scale the Himalayas to learn to meditate. Nor do you need to fast or punish yourself in order to benefit from meditation. True, people in monasteries may fast for days at a time, or they might sit still for long periods while being bitten by mosquitoes. But they can afford to challenge themselves with those discomforts because they don't have bills or children. It can be far easier to fast for a week than to go to work and care for your family day after day while you are exhausted or sick, much less trying to find time to sit still and meditate, too!

MEET "BRIAN" AND "MARIA"

Much of the activity in meditation is internal. It is interesting work, sometimes exciting, and even humorous. The inner activity of personal growth is not captured by lists of meditation instructions. It can only be observed by following the inner experiences of someone who is working on, sometimes struggling with, and eventually succeeding at the meditation practices.

In order to give you this perspective, we will introduce you to "Brian" and "Maria," whose stories appear throughout the book. Brian and Maria are amalgams of the hundreds of people we have taught. You will watch them as they practice the basic techniques and the applications. You will observe the intimate details of their struggles and successes. Brian's and Maria's internal monologues offer an intimate look at the inner experience of someone engaged in personal growth through the practice of meditation.

As you read Brian's and Maria's experiences, you will find them remembering comments from their teacher, which appear in bold text. This teacher is meant to be either of us, the authors. The teacher's comments contain tips that you will find helpful as you work with the techniques yourself.

BRIAN'S STORY

Brian is middle-aged, married, and has three children, ages seven to fourteen. He works full-time in a middle-management position. He finds his job stressful, and his doctor thinks the stress is contributing to his neck tension and high blood pressure. Brian has difficulties with angry verbal outbursts that have a negative effect on his home life, especially with his teenage son. He feels an ongoing sense of conflict with the world, and sometimes carries himself with a tense, irritable attitude. He is not happy with himself, and feels stuck, like his life is becoming a dead end. Brian has found himself asking the question "Is this all there is?" He would like to be different but he has no idea what to do. Everything seems to be out of his control. At times he feels sad and even hopeless. In addition to raising concerns about Brian's blood pressure, his doctor has suggested that Brian could be depressed.

Brian has at times expressed his frustration in conversations with his sister, Karen, a nurse. At one point she responded by looking at him very seriously and asking, "Are you willing to put some time and effort into changing, and do you have patience?"

Brian was surprised by her intensity, but replied, "I need to do something. There is no crisis now, but if things keep going this way, they will get worse."

"Well, then," she replied, "I suggest you start meditating."

"What!?" Brian exclaimed. "How is sitting around staring at my navel going to help me? I've tried relaxation and stress reduction, and they don't work for me."

"Look, Brian," she said, "you said you wanted a change. I'm telling you about something that will change *you,* more than you can imagine. Meditation is a lot more than relaxation or staring at your navel."

"I don't have time to meditate," he complained.

"Athletes and executives have used meditative techniques to become more effective. If they can make the time, so can you. Or," his sister bluntly stated, "if you don't want to do that maybe you can try antidepressants."

Brian drew a deep breath. "So what do I do? Where do I learn meditation?"

"There is an introductory session being held by a teacher I know," his sister replied. "I suggest you attend it. When you go, make sure you ask any questions you have. If meditation is going to work for you, it will need to make sense. So if something doesn't sound logical, ask about it."

MARIA'S STORY

Maria is a young and married with two small children. She also has a full-time job outside the home. She is being given more responsibilities at work and wants to move ahead there, but her family requires a lot of energy too. She is starting to feel the strain: having headaches, feeling tired a lot, and frequently feeling short-tempered.

Over the past couple of months, it's felt as if she's running on a treadmill, and that someone is continually increasing the speed. Her headaches have gotten worse and her doctor has prescribed medication for them. The medication decreases the pain, but it also sedates her. The sedation makes her feeling of being unable to keep up even worse.

One day she had lunch with an older friend and admitted, "Well, Susan, I just don't know. There is so much to do: the kids, my job, the household, my husband. It keeps piling up. I feel more and more scattered and stressed-out. I wish I could keep up and stay organized like you do."

Susan looked at her thoughtfully and said, "My secret to keeping up with everything is that I meditate. It's something you might try."

"But I don't have the time to meditate every day," Maria replied.

"I don't meditate every day. I meditate three times per week."

"But I don't even have time for that," Maria complained.

"If you meditate and become more efficient, you will gain more time than you spend," Susan replied. "For example, if you were able to reduce the amount of headache medicine you needed, you wouldn't experience the sedation that slows you down so much."

"Meditation can help my headaches?"

"People who practice meditation often have improvements in their physical condition," Susan stated.

"But I'm a Christian, and meditation is a Buddhist thing," Maria argued.

"Christians have been meditating for two thousand years. Meditation is a mental thing," Susan responded. "It's about learning to use your mind. Meditation has helped me a lot and I think it will be very helpful for you. I suggest you go to an introductory session. You can ask all the questions you want there."

Maria was skeptical, but since she saw Susan as a stable, practical person, she decided to attend the introductory session and see how she felt about it afterward.

HOW TO USE THIS BOOK

We've constructed this book to be your guide to this way of experiencing personal growth and inner peace. Even though we advise you to practice the techniques in the order we present them, we also encourage you to read ahead and find sections that interest you. You may wish to read the sections about Brian and Maria in each chapter, and share in their difficulties and successes. You may also wish to look at the comments and tips from their teacher that appear in bold text. Brian's and Maria's stories will give you a feeling for the process that occurs when ordinary people train their minds and achieve extraordinary results.

PART I

four practices for developing the five mental qualities

1 introduction

MEDITATION IS TRAINING FOR YOUR MIND

You can let your mind run automatically, or you can train your mind so it serves you more effectively. In this book, when we mention meditation, we are referring to mental exercises that improve the mind.

The four meditative exercises you will learn develop five primary mental qualities. These five mental qualities are *steadiness, flexibility, warmth, clarity,* and *spaciousness.* As you develop these mental qualities, you will find that your mind automatically performs tasks with greater ease. You become more adept at staying calm under pressure, adapting to new situations, working through conflicts, and finding creative insights. You become better at living, not just at meditating.

Learning meditation is like learning how to ride a bicycle. When you start learning to ride the bicycle, you feel awkward and fall frequently. So you practice, accepting the fact that you may fall. As you practice, your skill improves, you fall less often, and you can ride on busier streets. As you keep practicing, you are able to ride anywhere while feeling safe, and are able to handle emergencies as they arise. But in order to learn, you have to be willing to make some mistakes, and you have to try various techniques in order to find those that are effective.

In the same way, when you start practicing meditation, it is natural to feel awkward. You will have varying degrees of success. Sometimes you will have enjoyable experiences, and other times you will feel like you are practicing and getting nowhere. Continue to learn from your experience and you will improve.

WE TEACH BRIEF meditation techniques as well as extended techniques. The brief techniques require as little as ten seconds and no more than two minutes, and they are done throughout the day. Their purpose is to give you the experience of honing your mental skills in real-life situations.

These brief techniques are critically important. They allow you to make progress without spending large amounts of time sitting in meditation, to exercise your mind throughout the day. They also train you to apply meditation spontaneously and quickly in the real world.

GETTING STARTED: TIPS

Here are some tips that will help you learn meditation more easily. If you follow them, you will feel more comfortable practicing meditation and you will see results more quickly:

The Brief Techniques

Brief sessions last for about one minute. Unlike the extended sessions detailed below, they are to be done while you are engaged in your daily activities. The more often you practice the brief techniques, the faster you will make progress. You should practice the brief techniques during the "between times": the periods of time when you are not doing anything that requires your full attention. The following is a list of some of the between-times we or our students have found useful for practicing the brief techniques:

- Before and after meals
- Just after waking up, unless you are going to do an extended session then
- Just before falling asleep, unless you have just finished an extended session
- While walking from one room to another
- While walking out to the car
- Before driving or after driving
- While someone else is driving
- While going to the bathroom (yes, really)
- While washing up after going to the bathroom
- In the shower
- While waiting on "hold" during a phone call
- Before picking up a newspaper or magazine
- Instead of watching an advertisement on TV
- Before or after reading a book on meditation

If you use your creativity, you will find numerous times in which to fit a brief technique. The more often you do that, the faster you will progress.

Extended Meditation Sessions

Extended meditation sessions are to last fifteen minutes or longer. You will need to spend a total of at least ninety minutes per week in extended sessions to make consistent progress. You could practice fifteen minutes per day, six days per week. Or you could practice thirty minutes per day every Monday,

Wednesday, and Friday. Just try not to let more than two days pass between sessions.

If you spend more time in the extended meditation sessions, you will progress faster—but only up to a point. We do not recommend spending more than sixty minutes per day in extended meditation sessions.

As much as possible, try to practice the extended meditation sessions in the same place and at the same time of day. Doing so helps the extended sessions become a habit. On the other hand, it is better to practice at a different time or place than to skip a practice session. Pick a place that has a comfortable temperature and few disturbing noises. Good times to practice are early morning after waking, before lunch, just after work, or late evening before going to sleep. Sit in a posture that keeps your back fairly straight and allows you to feel comfortable without falling asleep. One popular posture is to sit in a chair with your feet flat on the floor. A second is to sit on a cushion on the floor with your legs crossed. A third is to kneel on a rug or carpet with your buttocks resting on your heels. Any posture is acceptable as long as it allows you to stay upright and comfortable for at least fifteen minutes.

IN EACH OF the brief and extended meditation techniques, there are three phases: *intention, execution,* and *reflection.* When most people think about meditation, they think only of the execution phase. But the intention and reflection phases are what improve your progress.

The first phase, *intention,* takes only an instant: you remind yourself of what you want to accomplish by practicing meditation. Your goals may be long-range, or more immediate. For example, in the Tibetan Buddhist tradition a common intention is "enlightenment for all beings." That is a long-range goal. You may be meditating to feel more at peace. That is a more immediate goal. Both are OK. The point is that by remembering your intention at the beginning of each practice session you learn much faster.

Once you have remembered your intention, you begin to practice the technique for that session. This is the *execution* phase of the session. The execution phase takes the most time and is what people think of as "meditating." It is the phase in which most of the work of meditation occurs.

The last phase is that of *reflection*. Its purpose is to give your mind time to integrate the experiences from the execution phase with your daily life. It is analogous to the "follow-through" described in athletic events. To do the reflection phase, remain quiet and remember any experiences from the session that stand out in your mind. Think about how those might relate to the goals that you focused on during the intention phase of the session. This will take a couple of seconds after a brief meditation technique, and may take up to a minute after an extended session. Reflecting on your experience reinforces the mental processes related to your goals, and makes the benefits of the meditation session easier to experience during the rest of the day.

TIME PRESSURE

Most people already feel too busy to meditate, and the thought of adding another activity to the day seems overwhelming.

One way to deal with the feeling of time pressure is to remind ourselves of the importance of meditating. One student described how she was lying in bed, feeling reluctant to get up and practice when the thought hit her, "You have a date with God and you're blowing him off!" We meditate to develop our mind, and thus improve our physical, mental, and spiritual

for how they work. You will also get a sense of which mental qualities you have in abundance, and which you need to strengthen.

STEADINESS AND FLEXIBILITY

Steadiness keeps your mind from wandering even in the presence of distractions. When your mind is steady, you can maintain the focus of your awareness and thinking, as well as remain in emotional states that you wish to prolong. Mental steadiness is also important because it helps you move toward goals in a consistent manner. People who can apply themselves to any protracted course of training, either physical or intellectual, have an abundance of mental steadiness.

Flexibility is the mental quality that helps your mind stretch and flow. While steadiness helps you maintain your mental focus, flexibility helps you to *change* that focus easily. It's not unlike flexibility in the body. When your body is flexible, you can change position easily and smoothly. When your mind is flexible, you can shift attention quickly and smoothly from one topic to another. You can also expand your awareness to encompass whatever you want to pay attention to. When your mind is flexible, your mental activity is smooth, relaxed, and unhurried.

The following examples demonstrate how steadiness and flexibility complement each other. If you are playing tennis, you not only have to keep your eye on the ball, you also have to stay aware of both your position on the court and your opponent's position. While doing all this, you must ignore all other distractions—for example, worries about performance or about people watching you. Steadiness helps you ignore distractions and keep track of the ball. Flexibility helps you to shift your awareness quickly and smoothly enough to keep track of your position and your opponent's position as well.

If you are driving and trying to shift lanes at a busy freeway interchange, you have to keep track of the car in front of you *and* look to the sides *and* in your mirrors to locate other cars. Flexibility helps you shift your attention rapidly from the front to the rear and to both sides. While you are shifting attention, steadiness helps you to keep track of the car in front of you so that you can avoid hitting it if it stops suddenly.

If you are giving a complex speech to an audience, it is normal to be anxious. But you also have to focus on your talk. Steadiness helps your mind to stay focused despite the anxiety. If members of the audience ask questions, you may have to shift topics to respond effectively to the questions. Flexibility helps you shift smoothly from one topic to another without getting confused.

Steadiness and flexibility are also important in relationships. For example, if you have children and feel tired when you return home from work, you need to be able to shift into a playful mood so you can interact well with your children. Flexibility helps you change from being tired to being playful, and steadiness helps you to ignore thoughts of work that try to intrude. You may be angry with someone and still need to listen to his or her position. Flexibility helps you disengage from your anger and shift into a neutral state. Steadiness helps you maintain that neutral state while you listen to the person's explanation.

Steadiness and flexibility work together so you can direct sustained attention and simultaneously keep track of other events. As you increase your steadiness and flexibility in a balanced manner, you will increase your ability to keep track of many tasks at once. You will be able to respond more easily to life's constant change. Steadiness is developed by centering and concentrating techniques taught in chapters 2 and 4. Flexibility is developed by attending techniques taught in chapter 3.

WARMTH AND CLARITY

Warmth and clarity are the next pair of mental qualities. Warmth is the quality that helps you accept things without prejudging them. It is directly related to tolerance and empathy. It is the quality that allows your mind to accept things it would otherwise reject automatically.

Clarity is the mental quality that helps your mind make distinctions and categorize. It helps you pick out details and distinguish one thing from another. It also increases your ability to analyze. A musician uses clarity to tune one instrument to another. A baseball umpire uses clarity to tell the difference between a ball and a strike. Clarity is especially valuable when you use it to notice the details of your own internal states: it helps you to know precisely what is on your mind.

Warmth and clarity complement each other. If you disagree with your spouse about something, you must be able to listen to her in an accepting manner even though you disagree. After all, until you have truly understood her, how can you discuss the issue intelligently? Warmth helps you listen to the ideas and emotions that your spouse is communicating. Clarity helps you to understand the details of your spouse's statements and how they relate to the current situation.

Warmth and clarity are very important because they allow you to be aware of your thoughts, emotions, or impulses, especially those with which you may be uncomfortable. If your teenage son comes home very late, you are likely to feel anger as he walks in the door. Warmth allows you to notice other emotions—for example, fear, disappointment, guilt, worry, or relief—that the anger might be masking. Clarity helps you understand how these emotions relate to the current situation. You might feel afraid that your son could have been hurt. You might feel disappointed that he didn't have the courtesy to call. You might feel guilty about being an inadequate parent. You might feel worried that your son was becoming irresponsible. And you would probably feel relieved that he was safe. Warmth helps you accept all the emotions that you feel. Clarity helps you identify them precisely and know how to deal with them.

Sometimes, you feel an emotion that does not seem to have been caused by a specific event. When this happens, warmth helps you be aware of the sensations and thoughts that you usually ignore. Clarity helps you to separate these sensations and thoughts and then evaluate their influence on your current mood. For example, if you are at work and the day is going reasonably well, you might find yourself feeling irritable, for "no reason." However, your irritation can come from a number of factors. You may not be getting things done as quickly as you'd like, or you may wish you were on vacation, or you may have had an argument with your child that morning, or you may simply be hungry. Warmth helps you to be open to unexpected factors that are related to your irritability. Clarity helps you to see precisely how each factor relates to your irritability. As a result, you can decide whether you should settle for doing a little less at work that day, start planning a vacation that evening, talk with your child when you get home, or get something to eat.

As you strengthen your warmth and clarity in a balanced manner, you will increase your ability to analyze several perspectives at once. You will be more accepting of others' ideas and at the same time understand how to explain your own. Warmth is developed by attending techniques taught in chapter 3, and clarity is developed by concentrating techniques taught in chapter 4.

SPACIOUSNESS

Spaciousness complements the other four mental qualities. It is experienced as a sense of freedom, of mental vastness. It enhances humor and creativity. When you have developed the quality of mental spaciousness, you experience a spontaneity at the newness of each moment. You also feel confident that you can handle difficult situations, not necessarily because you already know the answers, but because you know you can create solutions as you need them.

When your mind is spacious, you are able to let go of your usual ways of organizing information. This letting go allows you to find solutions to problems that appear impossible. Many brain teasers are designed to evoke this experience. Try to make six straight rows of dots with exactly four dots in each row. This sounds simple until you try it using only twelve dots. Or, try to connect nine dots arranged in a three-by-three grid, using four straight lines, without lifting your pencil from the paper. As you discover the solutions to these, you will have small but real experiences of mental spaciousness. Such experiences come from breaking the mental limitations that keep you from discovering a solution. That is why being told the answer does not have the same effect as finding the answer for yourself.

Spaciousness also helps you create constructive outcomes from negative situations. If a coworker makes a mistake, expressing frustration is a natural response; however, it is rarely constructive. Spaciousness helps you to step back mentally from the immediate effects of the mistake. Then you can find ways to turn the mistake into a constructive learning experience for you and your coworker.

Spaciousness can also help you at home. If your child tries to help you clear the dishes and drops them on the floor, an automatic response can be irritation, even though your child is only trying to help. Spaciousness helps you to step back and distance yourself from the mess at your feet. Your automatic response changes from irritation to a calmer "Oh well." Instead of being upset with your child, you both end up laughing together.

Spaciousness helps you let go of automatic ways of behaving and thinking so that you can discover new and creative options. As you increase your spaciousness and balance it with the first four mental qualities, you will find that you are more imaginative. You will become more humorous and more creative. Spaciousness is developed by opening techniques, taught in chapter 5.

The meditative practices we describe in part 1 are designed to develop these five mental qualities so you can use them effectively in daily life and use them to reduce stress. As you develop these qualities during your meditation practice, your reactions to life events will become more constructive and creative. These creative, spontaneous reactions will occur during routine events in your daily life, as well as during the unusual and more difficult situations that you encounter from time to time.

BRIAN'S REFLECTIONS ON THE INTRODUCTORY SESSION

Brian and Maria both attended an introductory meditation session. While they had different experiences of the class and different goals for meditation, by the end of the class each was enthusiastic about learning meditation.

On his way home from the introductory session, Brian reflects on his experience. One of the nice surprises was that the other people in the room all looked normal. Some were in sweats, some were in work clothes. There were even a few in business suits. "Hmm, this can't be all that weird," he had thought.

Brian found the idea of the five mental qualities interesting. As he thinks about them now, he can see examples of how they work in his life. He finds it quite easy to focus on things, and correctly decides he has a good deal of steadiness. He is also good at analyzing and picking out details. This comes from his mental clarity. However, he remembers numerous times when he was unable to change his focus or the way he was doing things. He has a reputation for being "stubborn" or "pigheaded." He also realizes that while he analyzes well, he has difficulty understanding others' perspectives. This has led to accusations that he is "closed-minded." He now realizes that those difficulties come from a lack of flexibility and warmth. He is pleased with his ability to focus and analyze, and realizes that he does not need to lose those. He simply needs to develop the complementary qualities, flexibility and warmth.

Spaciousness intrigues Brian and he recalls instances when he's had flashes of inspiration. He feels he could use a lot more spaciousness. He had asked the teacher if he should practice only the techniques that developed the qualities he thought he needed: flexibility, warmth, and spaciousness. **"That is a good question,"** the teacher had responded, **"People need all the mental qualities, and they need to be balanced. Start by practicing all the meditation techniques in the proper sequence so you will develop all the qualities in a balanced manner. Later, you may find you want to practice some techniques more than others, depending on the mental qualities you want to develop most."**

Brian particularly liked the emphasis on practical results. During one part of the session, the attendees were asked to think about what they would like meditation to help them achieve—that is, their goals or intended results from meditating. They were asked to write down one or two goals in each of four life areas: health, performance, relationships, and spirituality. The teacher said if they had questions about possible goals, they could speak to him during the break.

Brian's health goals were easy for him to pick. He knew about his health issues that were stress-related and it seemed that meditation could help with those. He decided that his health goals would be to reduce his neck tension and maybe even lower his blood pressure.

On the other hand, the performance goals that first came to Brian's mind seemed too big for him to have any hope of accomplishing. After a little reflection he decided to work on improving his golf game. He asked the teacher about this because it seemed a little odd to use meditation for that goal. His teacher smiled and said, **"Meditation doesn't have to be completely serious. It is OK to use it for lighter things. Applying meditation to your golf game will help you improve, and make it more relaxing for you. From that experience you will learn how to apply the techniques to other goals."**

Brian's relationship goal is to reduce the frequency and intensity of his verbal outbursts, both at work and at home, and especially with his children. While he is not violent, he does have a short temper and too often says things he wishes he hadn't. Brian was concerned that meditation would just make him ignore the situations that upset him. This would not be good because he does have to deal with those situations. He had expressed this worry to his teacher, who responded, **"Many people think meditation is about being calm and distant. That is incorrect. It is about being calm and present. You practice the basic techniques in solitude to train your mind to perform better at everything else you do. You become more effective at living."**

Brian was somewhat confused about the spirituality goal as he does not consider himself religious. When he asked his teacher about it, he was told, **"Being spiritual can be different from being religious. What do you want to live for that is bigger than you are, that seems**

holy or sacred?" Brian identified a sense of being at peace with people and the world as something spiritual. **"Fine, cultivating a deeper
and deeper sense of peace is certainly a spiritual goal, and one that
will benefit others as well as yourself."**

Brian feels pleased with the goals he has chosen. A part of his
mind seems very satisfied and happy, like a door is opening in a wall
that has been enclosing him. To be sure, meditation does not look
like a quick or magical fix. But in some way, that makes it seem even
more real.

MARIA'S REFLECTIONS ON THE
INTRODUCTORY SESSION

As Maria returns home from the introductory meditation class, she
reflects on the experience before calling her friend, Susan, to tell her
how it went. She realizes that it was not as strange or unusual as she
had been afraid it would be. The other attendees seemed to be regular people in regular clothing. The teacher was dressed casually and
looked no more mysterious than someone she might see in the
supermarket. She saw no sign that anyone was going to make her follow a different religion. In fact, the teacher was wholly accepting of
her goals, and her Christian beliefs.

Maria feels more able to accept herself after hearing the presentation on the five mental qualities. She finds it easy to go from one
thing to another. Having to change plans does not cause her any difficulties. However, often she has difficulty staying on a particular
course of action. She frequently changes plans even when she doesn't
have to, sometimes to the frustration of those around her. People
have called her "flaky," but she resents that because she likes her
ability to change easily. As she reflects on this, she concludes that her
ability to change easily is related to mental flexibility, and that her
flexibility needs to be balanced by more steadiness.

Maria also notes how open she is to new ideas or multiple ways of looking at a situation. However, she often jumps to a new idea before analyzing the first one. This has led to accusations that she is "superficial." She can now consider that this occurs because her natural warmth is not balanced by enough clarity.

Maria had just assumed these problems were part of her personality and would be with her forever. "That's just me," she used to say. Now she realizes that she is not "flaky" or "superficial." Those traits actually come from the presence of two valuable mental qualities, flexibility and warmth. She simply needs to balance those qualities with steadiness and clarity.

Maria likes the idea of having goals for her meditation practice. Her health goal was easy to pick: she wants to reduce the frequency and intensity of her headaches. They are bothersome, and while the medicine she takes for them helps reduce the discomfort, she does not like the way the pills make her feel. The teacher replied to her question about this, **"Meditation often helps reduce the frequency and intensity of headaches. You may even find that you are able to stop a headache before it starts. However, headaches, or any physical symptom, can be a warning sign from the body. So you need to work with your physician and let her know if the headaches do not improve."** Maria agreed to continue to see her doctor and to use the meditation to augment the medical treatment.

Her performance goal is to give better presentations at work. She tends to get nervous and easily flustered when speaking in front of other people, and would like to be more at ease. Her difficulty giving presentations is keeping her from moving ahead in her company. She was a little worried about using meditation to help her improve at something that is so connected with personal gain. When she brought this up with the teacher, he said, **"That is a good question. We want to make sure our goals are not just self-serving. Your goal is to improve your ability to communicate. That will help you and others. So using meditation to improve your ability to make presentations is an acceptable goal."**

Maria's relationship goal is to be more patient and less nagging at home. When something upsets her, she tends to complain about it more than is helpful. She knows she complains too much at times, but she can't seem to stop herself. Maria would like to be able to let go of things that are not important and to express dissatisfaction about things that matter in ways that get results.

Maria knew that her spirituality goal had to be related to her Christian faith. Her spiritual goal is to have a deeper relationship with God. She was a little concerned that meditation would not fit with that goal, that it was too Eastern to be used by a Christian. The teacher told her, **"Christianity has a long tradition of using meditation for strengthening one's personal relationship with God. You will certainly be able to use the meditation exercises you practice to become a better Christian."** Realizing that meditation techniques were a part of her Christian tradition helped Maria feel at ease.

WHAT DO YOU WANT TO GET OUT OF THIS?

Think about the four areas of your life: your health, your performance, your relationships, and your spirituality. Decide on one or two positive changes in each of those areas and write them down. You do not need to know exactly what you want, and it's OK to change your goals as you proceed through the book. Some suggestions for each of the areas follow:

Health
- Reducing minor ailments such as headaches or muscle tension
- Improving general health
- Making positive lifestyle changes

Performance
- Improving at a sport or other recreational activity
- Being able to complete a task faster or with less effort
- Learning a new skill

Relationships
- Decreasing anger
- Increasing patience and understanding
- Being gentler with others
- Being firmer at setting boundaries

Spirituality
- Deepening one's understanding of one's religion
- Developing a stronger connection with Spirit
- Finding more inner peace
- Becoming more loving

2 centering: putting your awareness into focus

IN THE NEXT four chapters we will introduce four basic meditative practices: centering, attending, concentrating, and opening. These four practices will develop the five mental qualities of steadiness, flexibility, warmth, clarity, and spaciousness. The basic meditation techniques emphasize one of these practices at a time. As you become familiar with the practices, you will be able to shift from one to another as needed. Before attempting these it is helpful to have some expertise with the basic techniques.

THE FIRST practice to become familiar with is centering. Centering teaches you to hold the focus of your awareness steady. Just like you need to be able to hold a camera steady in order to take photographs, you need to be able to hold your mental awareness steady in order to use other mental techniques. At first you may feel like the center of your awareness is wobbling, as if your mind were a camera being held by someone on a roller coaster. With practice you will be able to hold the center of your awareness steady as if your mind were a camera on a tripod.

To practice centering, pick something to be aware of. This is your *center of awareness,* or simply your center. It is possible to center on one of any number of things, such as the breath, or a word, or an image. Centering on different things can have different effects. As you become more familiar with centering, you can play with choosing different objects or sensations to center on.

The basic centering technique is to focus on the sensations in your lower abdomen as you breathe. As you do this, you will become aware of other sensations as well as thoughts. Simply allow all of these to be present and continue to focus on the sensations in your lower abdomen. If you find that your center has shifted elsewhere, simply return your awareness to the sensations in your lower abdomen.

There are good reasons for centering on the sensations in the lower abdomen. First, and most practically, those sensations are always present, so you can practice the technique anywhere. Second, centering on the lower abdomen tends to be relaxing. Third, it tends to promote a smooth, easy breathing pattern. This facilitates developing a calm, focused mental state.

Centering, however, is neither a relaxation exercise nor a breathing exercise. It is a mental exercise that teaches you to steady your mind, and it is a foundation for further meditative work.

PRINCIPLES OF CENTERING

Centering is the practice of placing your awareness on something, your center, and returning your awareness to that center if you are distracted. The *center* is whatever you're maintaining awareness of. Centering develops the mental quality of steadiness.

When your mind is centered, it is like a camera that is pointed at the subject of a photograph. The camera may wobble at bit, but if it drifts off the subject, the photographer readjusts the camera. In the same way, it is natural for your awareness to wobble somewhat. As long as you keep bringing your awareness back to your center, you are doing the practice correctly. Brian and Maria are both practicing a centering technique. For each, the center is the sensations in the lower abdomen. Let's follow them both through their experiences with centering.

BRIAN'S FIRST MEDITATION SESSION

It is 6:10 A.M., and Brian has just awakened for his first meditation practice session. He has decided to practice for fifteen minutes each morning. He figures that he will practice six days per week, and that will give him the ninety minutes per week that his teacher advised as a minimum. Getting up about fifteen or twenty minutes earlier than usual did not seem so difficult when he was thinking about it last night. Now he is not so sure. He feels a little stiff, and he is tempted to crawl back into his nice, comfortable bed. He shrugs off the temptation and pulls on a warm pair of sweatpants and a sweatshirt, and washes his face in cold water. Now somewhat awakened, he goes into the living room and, placing a pillow from the couch on the floor next to the wall, he sits down on it cross-legged.

Brian remembers that he is to start each session by thinking about his goals for meditation. **"Focus your intention at the beginning of each session,"** his teacher had said. **"That will increase your motivation and help you make faster progress."**

Brian thinks about his intention: "What am I up this early for, anyway?"

He reviews his long-range goals mentally: reducing his stress, improving his golf game, controlling his temper, and developing a sense of inner peace. He also remembers the immediate goal of this session: learning to steady his mind and maintain awareness of the sensations in his lower abdomen. Remembering these goals takes only a few seconds and completes the intention phase of the session. Brian then begins the execution phase.

He places his palms on his lower abdomen so that his thumbs are over his navel. He centers his awareness on the sensations in his abdomen under his palms. At first he feels nothing, and then he notices a little motion as he breathes in and out. He catches himself trying to change his breathing to make it deeper. He remembers his teacher's guidance: **"It's not a breathing exercise, it's a centering exercise. How fast, slow, shallow, or deep you breathe does not matter. Just be aware of the sensations."** Brian continues to notice the sensations of movement in his lower abdomen, and then begins to feel a sense of warmth there. After a couple of minutes he finds himself thinking about work. He tries to force these thoughts out of his awareness, but the thoughts seem to get louder. He is beginning to get frustrated when he remembers his teacher saying, **"It's OK to have other thoughts, so don't try to get rid of them; just tell them, 'Later,' or tell your thinking mind, 'Thank you for sharing,' and focus your awareness on your lower abdomen again."** Brian smiles. He begins to think "Later" as the thoughts about work arise. The thoughts subside, and he feels the comfortable warmth in his lower abdomen more clearly. After another couple of minutes, Brian notices that there is some tension in his neck. It's not getting worse, but it's certainly not going away. Immediately the thoughts start in again. "You're not relaxing, you're not doing it right, you might as well stop now! You'll never get this. You're wasting your time." His breathing speeds up a bit and he tenses in response to these thoughts. Again his teacher's words come to mind: **"It's _not_** a relaxation exercise, it's a mental exercise, a centering technique. You are training your mind. If you relax, great. If not, then you are *still* **training your mind and that is what counts."** As Brian remembers this, he is able to stop trying to relax. He returns his awareness to his lower abdomen. His tension stops building and instead eases. He settles down and feels more comfortable. After another couple of minutes, Brian hears the alarm on his watch go off, indicating it is time to stop the session. He is surprised: fifteen minutes have gone by already?

Before finishing the session Brian reflects on his experience. He notes how much noise his mind made. He remembers how hard it was to stay centered on the sensations and starts to criticize his performance. He then remembers his teacher saying, **"It is normal to have some difficulty at first. You are doing well if you keep bringing your attention back to the sensations in your lower abdomen."** Brian decides that while he did get distracted, he did pretty well at bringing his awareness back to his lower abdomen. After these reflections on his experience, Brian brings his awareness to his whole body, remembers the time and his surroundings, and then wiggles his fingers and toes a bit before he gets up to continue the rest of his day.

MARIA'S FIRST MEDITATION SESSION

Maria is getting ready for her first meditation session after her day at work. She has convinced her husband to watch the children during her meditation sessions three days a week. This will give her thirty minutes to practice on each of those days. He had balked a little at this, but assented when she told him it was to help her have more patience and fewer headaches. She changes out of her work clothes into something less constricting. She goes out into the garage with a blanket and gets into the front seat of her car. She feels a little silly doing this, but it really is the only place where she knows she will not be disturbed. She sits down in the front passenger seat, adjusting it so that she is comfortable. She then places the blanket over herself so that she feels warm.

As she starts the session, she remembers her teacher's words: **"Remind yourself of your intention as you begin each session by remembering your immediate and long-range goals. Answer the question 'Why am I spending my time doing this?' That will facilitate your practice."** Maria thinks about her goals for a minute: finding relief from her headaches, becoming more at ease giving presentations, feeling a greater sense of patience at home, and developing a deeper relationship with God. She also remembers her immediate goal for the session: keeping her mind focused on sensations in her lower abdomen and going back to those sensations if distracted. After remembering her intention, Maria begins the execution phase of the session.

She adjusts her position in the seat and places her hands in her lap. She centers her awareness on the sensations she is feeling in her lower abdomen. At first she can't feel anything, so she arranges her hands on her abdomen with her thumbs over her navel. This places her palms and fingers over her lower abdomen and then she is able to feel sensations there more clearly. Almost immediately she is hit by an urge to shift position. She tries to remain still; however, she becomes more and more uncomfortable. She doesn't understand how she can meditate if she can't even sit still for a few minutes. She remembers a comment from her teacher: **"Meditation doesn't mean sitting still, especially in the beginning. If you are feeling uncomfortable, shift position. If you have to move every couple of minutes, that is OK. Just shift position and then go back to what you are supposed to be practicing."** Maria allows her shoulders to wiggle some and she moves her legs back and forth. After doing this a few times, her need to shift decreases. Her body seems to have settled into position.

The first sensations Maria notices are a slight expansion and contraction in her abdomen as she breathes. She feels a little self-conscious about this but remembers what her teacher had said: **"Even though the air goes in and out of your lungs, your body has to make room for the air to come in. That means that your abdomen will expand a bit as you breathe in and will contract a bit as you breathe out."** The expansion and contraction feels gentle and peaceful, and Maria smiles a bit to herself.

As she continues to focus on her abdomen, Maria notices some warmth in her hands and then, under them, in her abdomen. At first the sensations are faint and she finds herself distracted numerous times. She wonders if she is doing the technique correctly. **"The key to centering is not how long you stay focused but training your mind to return to your center."** As Maria continues to recall her attention to the sensations in her lower abdomen, she finds the sense of warmth growing under her hands. Soon she begins to feel a pleasant sensation of warmth all through her lower abdomen. Her mind begins to drift off and suddenly she jumps, realizing she has almost fallen asleep. She opens her eyes and looks at her watch and is surprised to notice that twenty minutes have gone by. She remembers the instructions: **"Make sure you stay awake during the exercise. You can use meditation to go to sleep, but sleeping will not develop your mind like meditating."** She adjusts her position in the seat, closes her eyes, and goes back to being aware of the sensations in her lower abdomen. Her mind refocuses itself, and a short time later she hears her watch alarm go off.

She reflects on her experience. A lot of the distractions were thoughts from the day at work. She notes how calming it felt to let those thoughts go and return her focus to her lower abdomen. She remembers how she almost fell asleep and resolves to wash her face with cold water before the next session to make sure she stays awake. After these reflections, Maria brings her awareness to her whole body, reorients to time and place, wiggles her fingers and toes a bit, and then opens her eyes, feeling refreshed and calm.

INSTRUCTIONS FOR THE EXTENDED CENTERING TECHNIQUE

- Sit in a comfortable position in a place where you are not likely to be disturbed.
- Remember your intention by thinking about your long-range goals for meditation, as well as your immediate goal for the session. Your immediate goal for this extended centering technique is to maintain awareness of the sensations in your lower abdomen.
- Notice the sensations in your lower abdomen (below your navel). If you have difficulty sensing this area, place your hands on your abdomen with your thumbs on top of your navel and your palms against your stomach. In this position, your palms and fingers will rest on your lower abdomen. Notice that the lower abdomen includes the area to the sides and not just the front of the body.
- Breathe comfortably. There is no need to try to change your breathing pattern. Note that your breathing may vary naturally during the exercise.
- If you feel sleepy, then sit up straighter or open your eyes. If this is a consistent problem, then try washing your face with cold water before starting the session.
- You may still notice other things going on around you. If you get distracted, simply bring your awareness back to your center, the sensations in your lower abdomen. If you find yourself thinking about things, just tell the thoughts, "Later."

- It is OK to get distracted. The important thing is to learn to come back to your center.

Once you can maintain your focus on the sensations in your lower abdomen for about thirty seconds without straining or getting distracted, you are ready to move on. Depending on how much you practice, this usually takes from one to three weeks.

Remember, centering on the lower abdomen is just a beginning. As you practice other meditative techniques and applications, you will learn to center on other things in order to evoke other experiences.

BRIEF CENTERING PRACTICE: "RAPID RECHARGE"

The extended centering technique described above is to be done in extended practice sessions, which last at least fifteen minutes. By practicing the extended technique you will improve at centering, and your mind will become steadier. But if you practice *only* the extended technique, you will inadvertently teach your mind two things. First, your mind will get accustomed to always having fifteen or more minutes to get centered. It will not learn to center quickly. Second, you will teach your mind that centering is something that you do in the setting where you practice meditation, and nowhere else. So, if you only practice the extended technique, then you will severely limit your progress and reduce your ability to use the resulting steadiness.

The solution is to practice a brief centering technique several times *throughout* the day. These brief sessions should last no more than a minute. You should do at least five per day and they should be done in a variety of settings. Then your mind will learn to center quickly, anywhere and anytime you need it to.

A useful brief centering practice, called "Rapid Recharge,"

involves centering on a simple thought pattern for about thirty seconds. An effective thought pattern is the sequence "Calm – Relaxed." This helps the brief centering practice double as a stress-reduction exercise. You can try other thought patterns as well. Centering on different words may yield different results.

BRIAN'S EXPERIENCE WITH BRIEF CENTERING PRACTICE

Brian is sitting at his desk at work, preparing for a meeting later in the day. He is a little stressed about getting all his notes together. He suddenly hears his watch beep twice and realizes that an hour has gone by since he arrived. He thinks, "I don't have time for this," but then remembers his teacher's words: **"Brief practice is critically important if you really want to benefit from meditation. Also, taking a few seconds for it during work will often improve your efficiency."** Brian leans back in his chair and remembers his intention for meditation. He also remembers his goal for this technique, to center on a thought pattern for a few seconds. He closes his eyes and takes a deep breath as he thinks the word "Calm." He then releases the air as he thinks the word "Relaxed." He then breathes naturally, thinking "Calm" as he breathes in and "Relaxed" as he breathes out. After four or five breaths he reflects on the experience. He decides he does feel a little bit calmer and has a little less tension in his shoulders. However, the effect of the exercise is slight and he wonders if he is really succeeding at this. He again recalls his teacher's guidance: **"The results from brief practice are quite variable, especially in the beginning. Simply do the technique for a few seconds and accept the results, whatever they are."** Brian opens his eyes and goes back to working on preparing for his meeting. The whole practice session took less than a minute.

An hour later Brian's watch beeps again. He is still quite busy preparing for the meeting. He has promised himself he will do the brief technique at least five times per day. He decides that he will skip this time and practice it in one hour, just before his meeting.

That afternoon, Brian hears his watch beep again. He is feeling OK about how the meeting went earlier and feels happy about doing the brief technique. He closes his eyes, remembers his intention, and takes a deep breath as he thinks, "Calm," and then releases the air as he thinks, "Relaxed." He then breathes naturally as he thinks "Calm" on the inhalation and "Relaxed" on the exhalation. After a couple of breaths he is starting to feel calm and peaceful. He feels like continuing the practice because it feels so nice. However, he remembers, **"When doing brief practice you need to stop after a minute or two. If you lengthen the exercise beyond that, you will lose the effect of training your mind to respond rapidly."** Brian reluctantly decides to stop. He reflects on the experience and then opens his eyes.

Later, at the end of the work day, as Brian pulls his car into his garage and turns off the ignition, he is ready to head inside when he realizes that this is a perfect time to do the brief centering once again. But at the same time, he instantly notices how tired he feels and how much eyestrain he is experiencing. He settles back into the seat, closes his eyes and remembers his intention to center on a thought pattern for about a minute. He takes a deep breath as he thinks, "Calm," and releases the air as he thinks, "Relaxed." He continues to think "Calm" and "Relaxed" as he breathes easily. After several breaths he feels lighter, like he has released a load off of his shoulders. His neck feels looser, and his eyes are not as tired. He reflects on the experience and then goes inside, feeling more relaxed than he usually does when he arrives home.

MARIA'S EXPERIENCE WITH THE BRIEF CENTERING PRACTICE

Maria is busy at work. She has just hung up the phone and glances at a card she has taped to the wall. It reads "Calm – Alert." She remembers her commitment to do brief practice at least five times per day. Things are quiet right now, so she decides to practice. She sits up and reminds herself of her intention by remembered her goals for meditation. She also remembers her goal for this technique, to center on a thought pattern. Maria then keeps her eyes open as she takes a deep breath, thinking "Calm" as she does so. She then breathes out, thinking "Alert." Maria then breathes naturally, thinking "Calm" as she breathes in and "Alert" as she breathes out. After several breaths, she reflects on her experience. She notices that her head feels somewhat clearer and she feels less sleepy.

Later that morning Maria is walking down the hall to her supervisor's office. She suddenly remembers the card she taped to the wall and wonders if she could practice while walking. She remembers: **"Meditation is not just to be practiced sitting down with your eyes closed. The brief techniques are meant to be practiced in many situations. You should play with them and find ways to do them throughout the day. Just be careful about doing them when you need to be concentrating on something else, like when you are driving."** Maria decides now is as good a time as any to do the brief technique. So, while walking she remembers her intention. She then starts thinking "Calm" as she breathes in and "Alert" as she breathes out. After several breaths she stops and reflects on her experience. She feels a little different but is not sure just how. She then realizes that she is not quite as tense as she usually is when going to meet her supervisor.

After lunch, Maria is at a meeting and finds her attention starting to wane. She wishes that she were more alert and remembers her brief centering technique. She straightens her back a bit and thinks

"Calm" as she breathes in and "Alert" as she breathes out. After a couple of breaths, she feels more energized and the room seems to appear in sharper focus. She finds that she is able to pay attention to the presentation more easily.

That evening, Maria is getting her children ready for bed. They are tired, irritable, and quarreling. As she listens to them tease each other, she feels her patience wearing thin. Before she scolds them, she decides to use the brief centering exercise. She takes a deep breath and thinks "Calm," and then releases it as she thinks "Steady." She closes her eyes for a few breaths as she continues to center on the thoughts "Calm" and "Steady." Her irritation recedes, and she feels like she has a stronger connection with the earth, and is more grounded. She reflects that it is normal for tired children to quarrel, so she does not need to stop their minor squabbling but can instead focus on the solution, which is getting them into bed.

INSTRUCTIONS FOR THE BRIEF CENTERING PRACTICE: "RAPID RECHARGE"

As you can see, the brief centering technique is to be used in many different situations, and kept brief. Whether you do or do not feel any effect from the technique, you are to stop after a minute. This brevity teaches your mind to center quickly. By practicing in a variety of situations, you learn to use centering anywhere.

The instructions for the brief centering technique are as follows:

- Remember your intention: You are going to center on a simple thought pattern for about a minute. Recalling your intention should take only a second.

- Take a deep breath in as you think the word "Calm." Release the breath as you think "Relaxed." Then breathe freely as you continue to think "Calm" as you inhale, and "Relaxed" as you exhale.
- After about a minute (about ten breaths), reflect on the result.

Hints:
- You can do the technique with your eyes either closed or open.
- You can use other words to center on. We recommend that at first you use combinations such as the ones Brian and Maria used: "Calm – Relaxed," "Calm – Alert," "Calm – Steady."
- Be creative about finding times to fit the brief technique into the day. Common times to practice are: before and after meals; before or after driving somewhere (not while driving); before switching tasks; while doing routine tasks such as household chores; in the bathroom (instead of reading a magazine). You can also use an alarm or other signal to prompt you.

Practicing the brief centering technique at least five times per day will develop your ability to center quickly, enabling you to experience the benefits of mental steadiness throughout the day. Remember, the brief technique is at least as important as the extended technique.

BRIAN'S RESULTS FROM CENTERING PRACTICE

Brian is waking up for his morning centering session. He has been practicing for two weeks, and finds it easier to get up now. He washes his face with cold water to get fully awake, goes into the living room, and sits down on the cushion against the wall.

Brian closes his eyes and recalls his intention by thinking briefly about his goals for meditation. He also thinks about his goal for this session, centering on the sensations in his lower abdomen. He places his hands on his abdomen and focuses his awareness there. As is usual for him now, he notices the gentle movement of his abdomen as he breathes. Then he feels the sense of comfortable warmth there. Some thoughts come in about what he needs to do later in the day, but he is able to maintain his awareness of his lower abdomen. He feels a sense of comfort in his arms and shoulders. He gets distracted briefly by some thoughts about his car, an errand he needs to do, and a meeting at work. But after each distraction he is able to refocus his awareness on the sensations in his lower abdomen.

Brian's mind feels quiet and peaceful. He is aware of pleasant warmth in his lower abdomen and of a gentle sense of expansion and contraction as he inhales and exhales. He feels like a mountain, solid, steady, and connected with the earth. His face has a soft smile on it. The practice feels relaxed and natural. Again, he is surprised when his watch alarm beeps to signal the end of the session. He reflects on how comfortable the practice is for him and how easily he can refocus after getting distracted. He also thinks about how this practice has helped him start the day in a much calmer state of mind. He then returns his awareness to his whole body, reorients to time and place, and then stretches as his opens his eyes.

Later that day, Brian leans back in his chair at work, closes his eyes, and notices his breathing. He reminds himself of his intention to center on the thought pattern "Calm – Relaxed." He thinks "Calm" as he breathes in and "Relaxed" as he breathes out. He allows other thoughts to come and go, continuing to think "Calm" and "Relaxed." He allows his breathing rate to be natural and does not alter it or try to breathe deeply. He finds that after a burst of noisy thoughts, his mind gets quieter and his neck and shoulder muscles relax again. After ten or so breaths he reflects on his experience. He notices how sometimes the exercise evokes a definite sense of relaxation, while other times it seems to have little or no effect. He realizes that the positive effects have become more frequent as he has kept practicing over the past couple of weeks.

ONE NIGHT, BRIAN is having some difficulty falling asleep. He feels tired but can't seem to settle down. He decides to try using the centering technique to help him get to sleep. He lies on his back and places his hands on his lower abdomen. He then focuses on the sensations there as he thinks "Calm" and "Relaxed" over and over. Other thoughts are present, but gradually they fade into the background. After a few minutes, Brian feels his body loosen and his mind becoming more peaceful. A couple of minutes more and he feels warm and relaxed and his mind starts to drift. He rolls over onto his side, pulls the covers around him, and falls asleep.

Later Brian asked his teacher if this was OK. His teacher responded, **"You can certainly apply centering to help you get to sleep. Meditation is meant to be used. You combined elements from the extended technique and the brief technique to suit your intention. And it worked. Good job."**

AFTER TWO WEEKS of practice Brian is pleased with his progress. He enjoys the extended practice. It is a good way to start the day. The brief practice is particularly useful for him. He finds that doing it frequently keeps his stress level down throughout the day. If he forgets to do it on a particular day, he notices a definite increase in tension. When he does use the brief technique, not only is his stress level lower, but he is also able to shrug off minor annoyances. He gets less upset while driving and is more relaxed around the house. Using the centering technique to get to sleep is a bonus. Brian is looking forward to the next practice, *attending*.

MARIA'S RESULTS FROM CENTERING PRACTICE

Maria is sitting in her car preparing to do the extended centering exercise. She has been practicing for about two weeks and feels less self-conscious about it now. Practice is becoming more routine. She adjusts the blanket over her, places her palms on her lower abdomen, and closes her eyes. She thinks briefly about her goals for meditation and focuses her awareness on the sensations in her lower abdomen.

After a few seconds, she finds herself thinking about her day at work and realizes she has lost track of the sensations in her abdomen. She refocuses her awareness on the sensations of movement there. Then she gets distracted by an itch on her leg. She scratches it and refocuses on her lower abdomen. She continues to get distracted every few seconds for several more minutes, but after each distraction, she simply refocuses her awareness on her lower abdomen.

Gradually she begins to feel a sense of comfortable warmth in her palms. As this sense of warmth spreads into her abdomen, the distractions become less frequent. However, she still gets distracted at least every minute. Sometimes the distractions are sensations, but most of the time they are thoughts about the house, her husband, her children, or her work. She wonders if she is doing the technique correctly and remembers, **"Many people find they get distracted frequently during centering practice. The purpose of centering is to develop enough mental steadiness so you can do the more complex meditative practices. Once you can maintain your awareness of your center for twenty to thirty seconds, and can refocus your awareness easily when distracted, you are doing well enough."**

Maria realizes that even remembering this is another distraction, but it relieves her performance anxiety and she is able to refocus on the sensations in her lower abdomen. When her timer goes off, Maria reflects on her experience. The exercise is calming, but not as settling as she thought meditation was supposed to be. She worries that if she has this much difficulty with the first practice, then she will find the other practices impossible. She had complained about this to her teacher, who responded, **"If your mind is jumping around during the centering sessions, it may be because it has a lot of natural flexibility. If that is so, you will find the next practice, attending, to be a lot easier than centering. Just because a practice comes later in the sequence does not mean that it will be more difficult."** Maria accepts the fact that her mind likes to jump around. She is able to maintain awareness of the sensations in her abdomen for thirty seconds at a time. She is therefore ready to move on to the next practice, attending.

The next day, Maria pushes back from her chair at work and looks out the window. She remembers her intention to center on the thought pattern "Calm – Alert." She wants to be able to remain calm while also keeping her eyes open and staying aware of her surroundings. She thinks the word "Calm" as she inhales and thinks the word "Alert" as she exhales. She notices that her breathing seems to deepen a bit and she sits up a little straighter in her chair. After a few more breaths, she feels as if her vision is sharper and more focused. She also feels a sense of strength in her body, as if her muscles are toned and ready for action. After about a minute she stops centering and reflects on her experience. She notices how the sense of being calm and alert is different from her usual state during the day, and that it is getting easier to focus her mind.

AS MARIA REFLECTS on her meditation practice so far, she has mixed feelings. She finds the extended practice helpful because she can let go of the events from work before being with her family. This improves her interactions at home, but the extended sessions are not quite as restful as she had hoped they would be. On the other hand, the brief practice is especially useful for her. When she is starting to feel like too many things are demanding her attention at once, the brief practice helps her stay calm and helps keep her from getting scattered. She can use the technique anywhere: walking down the hall, before and after driving, even during conversations. Sometimes she finds herself thinking "Calm – Alert" spontaneously, even before she realizes she is getting upset. This is a positive change in her life and she is hoping the next practice, *attending*, will be just as useful.

REVIEW OF CENTERING

Centering trains you to keep your awareness steady. What you are aware of is called your *center*. You can center on a variety of physical or mental objects. The basic techniques described in this chapter involve centering on the sensations in your lower abdomen, and centering on a simple thought pattern.

While you are centering, you may also be aware of other sensations or thoughts. If you lose awareness of your center, simply bring your awareness back to it.

Centering is to be practiced in extended sessions of at least fifteen minutes for a total time of at least ninety minutes per week. It is also to be practiced in brief sessions of up to one minute several times per day.

Once you can maintain awareness of your center for thirty seconds without being distracted, then you are ready to move on to the next practice, *attending*. This usually takes only one to three weeks of practice, especially if you practice both the extended and brief exercises.

Remember, the brief practice sessions are at least as important as the extended practice sessions. In fact, as Maria experienced, you may get more noticeable benefits from the brief sessions than you do from the extended sessions. Each reinforces the other, so practice both!

TIPS FOR THE PRACTICE OF CENTERING

- Recall your intention at the start of each session by reviewing your goals for meditation. This takes only a second or two.
- Comfort is important. Make sure you are warm and that you are sitting comfortably. If you want to move or shift position during the session, that is OK. For example, if you have a cold and need to blow your nose during the session, just do so and return to centering.
- Stay awake during the sessions. It can help if you wash your face with cold water at the beginning of the session.
- The brief practice is extremely important. You can do it before and after meals, after driving, on the bus, while using the bathroom or taking a shower, before starting a task, after finishing a task, and at other similar times throughout the day.
- You can also use centering to fall asleep at bedtime. Simply center on your lower abdomen while thinking "Calm – Relaxed" after you lie down in bed. It is OK to use centering for this purpose. It is a simple and effective application of meditation.

3 attending: developing your mind's flexibility and warmth

NOW THAT YOU have some familiarity with centering, we want to introduce the second meditation practice, *attending*. Attending develops your mind's flexibility and warmth. As you practice attending, your mind will move more quickly and you will be able to keep track of more things at once. You will also be more receptive and aware of what is going on around you and inside you.

When you are attending, your mind is like a camera with a wide-angle lens: though it is centered on something, you are at the same time aware of what is going on *around* that center. When something distracts you, you identify it as precisely as possible. Then you disengage from the distraction and move your awareness back to your center. We use the word "disengage" instead of "let go" here because many times you need to exert some effort to get away from what is distracting you. If the distraction has grabbed you, passively letting go will not help you.

Recalling the camera analogy, attending is like picking something for the center of the photograph and then using a wide-angle lens. Other things appear in that wide-angle view, but you keep the camera centered on the subject of the photograph. If something distracts you and you happen to swing the camera toward it, you simply notice that you have shifted the camera and then recenter the camera on your original subject. In the same way, in order to attend to something, you keep your awareness centered on it, and notice what else shows up. If your awareness shifts away from your center, you identify what distracted you and then return your awareness to your original center.

Attending enables you to influence your experience of the "now." The "now" is quite complex. Is the "now" the memories you are having, the sensations you are experiencing, the thoughts you are thinking, or the emotions you are feeling? If you reflect on the distressing scenes you see in the nightly news, your "now" will be different than if you reflect on the loving things people do for one another. Attending techniques help you understand how your mind chooses which "now" to experience. Eventually you will be able to influence that choice and experience a "now" that is peaceful.

The basic attending practice is to center on the sensations in your nose or mouth as you inhale and exhale. You then notice other sensations, thoughts, or emotions that accompany these sensations. When you start attending, you may be surprised at the sensations and thoughts that show up as distractions, especially the thoughts. Some may not be ones you will be proud of. You will think, "Did I really think that?" It is important simply to accept the distressing thoughts and disengage from them without blaming yourself or feeling guilty.

One of the other things you will notice is that thoughts, sensations, and emotions have a life of their own. They will arise and disappear spontaneously, and one will lead into another without any input from you. This teaches you how much of what you consider your "self" is really just a number of programmed reactions. As you become aware of these, you gain the ability to change them. You can respond instead of react.

Attending differs from centering because when you are attending, you identify the distractions precisely instead of ignoring them. Also when you are attending, your goal is to identify other phenomena, not just to stay aware of your center. Attending trains your mind to go out, touch something, and then come back. This builds mental flexibility and quickness. And when you identify thoughts or feelings that you would rather ignore, you develop tolerance.

Basic attending skills can be developed in a few weeks. However, because attending gives you enormous amounts of information about your mental processes, it can continue to benefit you indefinitely.

BRIAN'S FIRST EXPERIENCE WITH ATTENDING

Brian sits down for his morning meditation session. Today he is starting a new practice, attending. He was doing well at centering, and his teacher told him, **"Once you can center for about thirty seconds without getting distracted, you are ready to move on to attending."** Brian remembers his goals for meditation, and the immediate goal for this session: to center on sensations in his nose while identifying and disengaging from distractions.

He notices the sensations of air moving in and out of his nose, the sense of coolness as he breathes in, and the sense of warmth as he breathes out. These sensations are faint, and he finds them a little difficult to keep track of. He suddenly gets distracted by an itch on his leg. He identifies the sensation as an itch and disengages from it by moving his attention back to the sensations of air moving in and out of his nose. Almost immediately he feels the itch again. He again identifies the sensation, and brings his awareness back to the air moving in and out of his nose. Again the itch distracts Brian, and he feels frustrated. He identifies his experience as "frustration," and goes back to the sensations of his breath. The itch returns, and Brian identifies it and goes back to his breath. He wonders if he is getting anywhere. He identifies *this* as "a thought" and goes back to the sensations of his breath moving in and out of his nose. The itch returns. Brian remembers, **"It is OK to move or shift position to relieve discomfort, especially when you are beginning. Just make sure, before you shift or scratch or whatever, that you have identified what is causing you to want to move. As your skill improves, you will be better at disengaging from distractions and that will keep you from getting frustrated."** Brian identifies the itch and then moves his hand and scratches it. He feels a sense of relief and then goes back to focusing on the sensations of air moving in and out of his nose.

Brian figures he has been sitting for less than two minutes and already he feels exhausted. He remembers the sense of peace he felt from centering and wonders if attending is going to be of any use to him. **"Attending can take more effort than centering. Therefore it may feel more tiring, especially at first. It is a critically important practice because it develops mental flexibility, the ability to identify and disengage, and the ability to contain emotions. If you only practice centering, you may feel relaxed, but you will not make much progress."**

Brian identifies these thoughts and moves his awareness back to his breath. He continues to be distracted every couple of seconds and can't believe how much noise his mind makes. He remembers a comment from his teacher: **"Most of our mental noise goes** unnoticed. **When you first start to practice attending, you are often surprised by how noisy your mind really is."**

After a couple more minutes Brian is feeling a sense of mental fatigue. He is wondering if he should stop meditating. **"When you are feeling fatigued with a practice, you should exert effort, but not strain yourself. If you are feeling strain, then move to an easier practice. If you are feeling tired from attending, go back to centering for the remainder of the session. That is better than stopping your session early."**

Brian identifies these thoughts and decides that he has expended enough effort for today. He shifts his attention from the sensations of air moving in and out of his nose to the sensations in his lower abdomen. After a couple of breaths, he feels the usual sense of calm return, and the distractions subside.

Soon his alarm beeps and he reflects on his experience. Attending takes more effort than centering; his mind has to work differently to identify and disengage from distractions. He is also surprised at how much noise his mind makes. He has a sense that he will be learning a lot from this practice. Brian then brings his awareness to his whole body, remembers the time and place, and stretches his arms and legs as he opens his eyes.

MARIA'S FIRST EXPERIENCE WITH ATTENDING

Maria has practiced centering for two weeks. It has remained somewhat difficult for her after her initial success, but she can now maintain continued awareness of the sensations in her lower abdomen for about thirty seconds before getting distracted. She wondered if she had made any real progress, but her teacher said, **"You are doing fine. Once you can maintain continuous awareness of your center for twenty to thirty seconds without getting distracted, you are ready to move on to attending."**

Maria arrives home, changes out of her work clothes, goes into the garage, and sits in her car as she has done before. She adjusts her blanket over her, closes her eyes and remembers her intention for the session. She remembers her goals for meditation and then thinks about the immediate goal for this session: identifying distractions and disengaging from them while she centers on the sensations of air moving in and out of her nose.

The first thing Maria notices is that her nose is a bit stuffy and it feels hard to breathe through it alone. The distraction is obvious; she can't get enough air. It is difficult to disengage her awareness from the sensation that she is suffocating. **"If your nose is stuffed, or if it feels congested, then breathe through your mouth. Center on the sensations of air moving across your lips instead of the sensations of air moving in and out of your nose."**

Maria opens her mouth slightly and manages to breathe more easily. She notices the coolness of the air as it flows in and the warmth as it flows out. After a couple of breaths, Maria realizes that she is thinking about work. She identifies those thoughts and disengages from them by deliberately bringing her awareness back to the sensations of air moving across her lips. She then feels tingling in her left foot. She identifies it and disengages her awareness from it, moving her awareness back to her lips. The tingling fades. Maria then senses how the coolness at her lips seems to flow inward through her mouth and down into her lungs as she inhales. She begins to have a sense of the air flowing into her whole body. A comment from her teacher comes to mind: **"When you start to practice attending, you want to center on something specific. Restrict your center to the sensations in your nose or your lips. Do not focus on the sensations of the air moving through your body. Simply identify them as other sensations and go back to centering on the sensations of air flowing through your nose or over your lips."**

Maria brings her awareness back to the sensations of air moving across her lips. She again gets distracted by thoughts about work.

She identifies these as "thoughts about work" and moves her awareness back to her lips. Then she remembers that one of her children had asked her to buy something for her, and she had forgotten about this. She recognizes this as a thought and again centers her awareness on the sensations of air moving across her lips. The thought comes back immediately, and she identifies this as a "thought about forgetting" and places her awareness on the sensations at her lips. She begins to feel upset and identifies this as "feeling upset," and goes back to her breath. Then she feels her shoulders tighten. She notices this sensation and goes back to centering on the sensations of air moving in and out of her mouth. Then the thoughts return about forgetting to purchase the item and how her child will react.

Maria feels like she is getting beaten up by the thoughts about having forgotten to buy the item for her child. She remembers a suggestion from her teacher: **"If you are getting bombarded by distractions related to the same topic, then one way of disengaging is to say 'Later' or 'Thank you for sharing' to your mind after you have identified the distractions. That tells your mind that you will deal with them, but that you have more important things to do right now."**

Maria finds herself thinking about her child's reaction. She identifies those thoughts, thinks "Later," and goes back to the sensations at her lips. This seems to quiet her mind a bit. She is able to stay centered on her breath for a little while and then the thoughts about forgetting the item for her child return. She recognizes these and again thinks "Later." The thoughts go away and Maria is able to return her awareness to the sensations of air moving across her lips.

Maria feels a little tired from the experience, but she also feels a sense of relief from having quieted the thoughts about her child. A feeling of calm and peace comes over her and she is able to keep her awareness on the sensations in her mouth as she breathes. She continues to identify distractions as they arise and return her awareness to her breath in a calm manner until she hears her watch alarm beep.

As Maria reflects on her experience, she first notices that it seemed easier to identify the distractions in this attending practice than to ignore them the way she did in her centering practice. She is also pleased at how thinking "Later" seemed to quiet her mind. Finally she realizes that she feels much calmer about having forgotten the item for her child and will be able to handle her child's disappointment more peacefully. Instead of berating herself for being forgetful or uncaring, she can simply accept the situation and apologize calmly. Maria then brings her awareness to her whole body, reorients to her time and place, and wiggles her fingers and toes a bit as she opens her eyes.

PRINCIPLES OF ATTENDING

Practicing attending will teach you to identify and disengage from mental phenomena. The basic attending technique builds on centering, but during centering practice, you ignore distractions. If you lose the awareness of your center, then you simply move your awareness back to it. During the attending practice, you identify distractions clearly, and then disengage from them and go back to being aware of your center.

In order to identify a distraction, you accept the fact that your awareness is not on your center. You do not try to hold on to your center. You accept the distraction into your awareness and simply classify it as a thought, a sensation, or an emotion. By accepting the distraction without fighting it you develop the mental quality of warmth. Your mind becomes more accepting of phenomena.

Identify the distractions simply. Do not analyze them. You'll only need to distinguish between thoughts, sensations, and emotions at first. Many people find they can identify the distractions more precisely than that, and as long as you are not analyzing the distractions, you may do so. Brian labeled a sensation as an itch, and Maria was able to notice a thought about her child. However, both Brian and Maria made those identifications immediately. They did not have to dwell in their experiences to identify their respective distractions.

After identifying a distraction, you need to disengage from it and move your awareness back to your center. This deliberate movement of your awareness develops mental flexibility.

Often, disengaging from a distraction will require some effort. It is more active than simply "letting go." The distractions grab your attention, the way a thornbush grabs clothing. Letting go does not remove the thorns from your clothes, nor does letting go remove the distractions from your experience. To remove the thorns, you need to notice each one and work it loose from your clothing. To disengage from distractions, you need to deliberately identify each one and work your awareness away from it. This takes practice.

One way to disengage from the distractions is to simply exert mental effort and move your awareness back to your center. If the distractions keep returning, then saying "Later" in your mind can help. You're letting your mind know that you are aware of whatever issue keeps cropping up, and will get to it in time.

If the distraction is an uncomfortable sensation, it is OK to disengage from it by moving or shifting your body to relieve the discomfort. Just make sure that you have identified the sensations and that you move deliberately, with awareness, instead of reacting automatically.

Distractions can be thought of as being like a net with a lot of fishhooks attached. If you do not see the net coming, then by the time you notice it, the net may be wrapped around you, and you will have several hooks embedded in you. If you notice the net coming quickly, you can deflect it before any of the hooks have sunk into you. Then you do not get caught by it. The following story illustrates this.

I, Joe, was starting a meditation session at about 11:00 P.M. I had planned to do a rather complex practice, so I had waited until the house was quiet so I wouldn't be disturbed by noise. As soon as I started, a neighbor's dog began to bark. The sound was very distracting and I quickly became quite irritated, first at the dog and then at the neighbor, who was not doing anything to stop the noise. I identified the emotions as irritation and frustration, and moved my awareness back to what I wanted to practice. Then the dog barked again, distracting me. I identified this, but then reexperienced the angry thoughts and irritation. I kept trying to disengage from them, but the irritation and thoughts returned with a vengeance.

Since I was having difficulty disengaging from those emotions, I speeded up my mental awareness to identify the distractions more quickly. The most obvious distraction was the dog barking; however, I realized that was not a sensation but a perceptual conclusion. I really had no proof that there was any dog barking. It could have been a car stereo outside playing the sound of a dog barking. So I worked on being more precise. As I did so, I became aware that the distraction was some kind of sensation in my ears that came and went and rose and fell. There was, in effect, no bark and no dog. The sensation, perceived in this new way, was quite easy to disengage from. I was able to continue the practice as I had intended.

By learning to identify and disengage from distractions, you develop mental flexibility and warmth. In this basic attending technique, you train yourself to identify and disengage from distractions while centering on the sensations of air moving in and out of your nose. When you center on the sensations in your nose, you are not stimulating your mind to produce any particular distractions. If you center on other things, the distractions will often be different. In part 2, where we describe applications of meditation, you will see how attending while centering on other things generates more specific thoughts, sensations, and emotions that lead to insight into your life.

INSTRUCTIONS FOR THE EXTENDED ATTENDING TECHNIQUE

- Sit in a comfortable place where you are not likely to be disturbed. It is OK if there are some distractions, as distractions are useful in your attending practice.
- Focus your intention by thinking about your long-range goals for meditation, as well as your immediate goal for the session. Your immediate goal for this exercise is to center on the sensations of air moving in and out of your nose while you identify and disengage from distractions.
- Notice the sensations of air moving in and out of your nose. Keep your awareness on the sensations in your nose and do not follow the sensations of air moving inward. The most obvious sensations are a sense of coolness as you inhale and warmth as you exhale.
- Breathe comfortably. There is no need to change your breathing pattern. Note that your breathing pattern may change during the exercise.
- If you get distracted from the sensations in your nose, identify what distracted you. To identify the distraction, notice the distraction enough so that you can recognize it. There is no need to use mental descriptions of the distraction or to talk to yourself about what it was. You have identified the distraction if you could describe it quickly if someone shook you by the shoulder and asked what distracted you. The distraction is typically a sensation, a thought, or (less commonly) an emotion.

- After identifying the distraction, disengage your awareness from it by moving your attention back to the sensations of air moving in and out of your nose, your center.
- Disengaging from the distraction may take some effort. One way of disengaging is to simply refocus your awareness on the sensations in your nose after identifying the distraction. This will work for most distractions.
- If the same distraction keeps returning, then telling it "Later" after identifying it can help you disengage from it.
- Identifying the distraction as quickly as possible will also help you disengage from it.
- Another way of disengaging is to identify the activity your mind is doing, instead of identifying the content in your mind. For example, if you are having difficulty disengaging from a thought, you can recognize that activity as "thinking," instead of identifying the content of the thought. Recognizing the activity separates you from the content of the thoughts, making it easier to disengage from them. In the same way, if you are being distracted by sensations, you can identify the activity as "sensing," and if emotions are causing the difficulty, you can recognize that activity as "feeling."
- Continue to identify distractions and return your awareness to your center for the rest of the exercise.
- It is very important to identify distractions without labeling them verbally. As you let go of verbal mental activity you will notice the incredible speed of the flow of sensations. The difference between sensations and verbal descriptions of sensations is like the difference between an action movie and a verbal commentary on the movie.

When you practice this technique, you may find yourself distracted every couple of seconds. That is normal. Simply continue to identify and disengage from the distractions. If you begin to feel too tired, then stop attending and simply center on the sensations in your lower abdomen. That will be more peaceful. Remember, your endurance will increase with practice.

Before you end the session, reflect on your experience. After the session, you may want to make notes about any distractions that seemed important. For now do *not* try to make such notes during your session.

When you can identify distractions and disengage from them without straining for two to three minutes out of the fifteen-minute session, then you are ready to add the next practice, *concentrating*.

BRIEF ATTENDING PRACTICE: "HOW DID I GET HERE?"

The extended attending technique described above is to be done for at least fifteen minutes at a time. There is a brief technique to increase attending skills that should be practiced as well. This brief technique is incredibly useful and will increase your understanding of how your mind works. It takes less than thirty seconds and can be done anytime and anywhere, except while operating machinery.

To do the brief technique, you ask yourself, "How did I get here?" You then pay attention to what has been going through your mind for the last couple of minutes. After spending about twenty seconds reviewing the thoughts, sensations, and emotions you have experienced over the last couple of minutes, you stop the technique and go on with your activity.

You should do this technique several times per day. You may be surprised at some of the patterns that run through your mind on a regular basis, even when you are not feeling particularly emotional. Still, the technique is quite useful if you are feeling upset, anxious, fearful, or sad. It will help you to get ideas about how to handle your negative emotions in a constructive manner.

Remember, this is a *brief* technique. It should take you only a few seconds to review the last couple of minutes of your experience. If you are spending more than that, then you are getting too analytical, or reviewing too far back in time. Keep it short.

BRIAN'S EXPERIENCE WITH BRIEF ATTENDING PRACTICE

Sitting at his desk at work, Brian suddenly realizes that his neck is feeling stiff. He remembers, **"The brief attending technique is to be practiced frequently throughout the day. It is especially good to practice if you notice yourself feeling tense or upset."** Brian decides to practice, as he is definitely tense for some reason. His intention is to be aware of his experience and where it comes from. He asks himself, "What is going on?" He tunes in to his current experience and notices the tension in his neck and shoulders. As he does this, he thinks about what has happened over the last couple of minutes. He remembers that he had just seen a message from his supervisor in his morning e-mail. He remembers that he then thought about a project he was a little behind on. His mind had jumped to the conclusion that the message was going to be asking him for an immediate report on the project. He then remembers that his shoulders and neck tensed as he thought about how he would have to explain why he was a little behind on the project. Brian reflects that his tension is related to a conclusion he has made without any actual data. The whole technique took about ten seconds.

Brian decides to look at and deal with the memo now instead of worrying about it. As he reads it, he realizes that it is just a reminder of a meeting he is to be at later that day. Brian laughs to himself and feels his neck and shoulders relax a bit. He decides it would be a good idea to take a minute and relax. He closes his eyes and does the brief centering practice he enjoys, thinking "Calm" as he breathes in and "Relaxed" as he breathes out. After a minute, he reflects on how comfortable he feels and how much more energy he seems to have. He returns to his work with a sense of satisfaction.

Several hours later, Brian is walking down the hall at work toward the copy machine. He feels curious about what is on his mind and decides to do the brief practice. He sets his intention to pay attention to what is going on in his mind. As he checks in with himself, he realizes he is thinking about an upcoming basketball game. Reflecting upon his thoughts over the last minute, he realizes he started thinking about a game he had watched on TV last week and then began thinking about the upcoming game, wondering who would win, given what he had seen last week. There doesn't seem to be any particular reason for thinking about the games, his mind was just doing it spontaneously. He reflects on the experiences and decides, correctly, that this was just some random noise going through his mind and it does not have any particular meaning. The brief session takes about fifteen seconds. He finishes it as he gets to the copy machine.

Several days later Brian is at home after work, and has to deal with some squabbling between his children. He suddenly realizes that he feels very irritable. He remembers his intention to be aware of his experience and asks himself, "How did I get here?" He notices a series of angry thoughts about his family not appreciating him. As he becomes aware of his sensations, he realizes that his physical energy is low and that he feels a little light-headed. He suddenly remembers that he skipped lunch to get more work done. He reflects on the fact that maybe this has something to do with his being irritable. Brian tells his children that he will be right back. After washing his face and having a glass of juice, his head feels much clearer and he has more energy. He returns to the conflict between his kids without getting angry.

MARIA'S EXPERIENCE WITH BRIEF ATTENDING PRACTICE

Maria is driving to work when she suddenly notices that she is anxious. While at a stop light, she decides to do her brief attending practice. She sets her intention to be aware of what is going on in her mind. She asks herself, "What's happening?" She notices her anxiety and then realizes she is thinking about getting a ticket. She suddenly remembers that she just a saw a police car pull out from a side street. Maria is surprised at how simply seeing a police car made her so nervous. She starts to think about that, but remembers, **"When you do the brief practice, you will be amazed at some of the things your mind comes up with. Don't try to analyze them. Just notice them and keep the practice short."** Maria reflects that she has been driving well and so is in no danger of getting a ticket. She also decides to pay some extra attention to her driving. The light turns green and she moves on.

Later, Maria is walking out of the office, on her way to lunch. She decides to do the brief attending technique and asks herself, "What am I thinking?" She realizes she is thinking about gardening. She then remembers her experience over the last couple of minutes. When she left her work, she had noted it was a nice spring day. Then she had seen buds on a tree, and heard a bird chirping. That made her think about winter being over and spring being a time for planting, which led to her thoughts about gardening. As she reflects on this, she notes that this thought sequence was just a natural response to her environment. As the thoughts are pleasant, she continues to think about the garden she wants to plant while she walks the rest of the way to lunch.

A couple of days afterward, Maria senses a headache coming on. She decides to check in with herself and asks, "What's my experience?" She notices the sensations in her head, and then notices some thoughts about a friend at work concerning a disagreement that the two of them had recently. Maria realizes that these thoughts about the disagreement came up during several brief attending sessions over the last couple days. She reflects on how she needs to work on reaching an understanding of her friend's position. She decides to call her friend that afternoon to schedule some time to talk. As Maria finishes the brief practice, she notices that her body feels different. She head feels a bit more comfortable. Since she does feel a little discomfort, she decides to take a mild pain reliever to prevent any more symptoms from developing.

INSTRUCTIONS FOR THE BRIEF ATTENDING PRACTICE: "HOW DID I GET HERE?"

The brief attending practice of "How did I get here?" is incredibly useful and develops the mind rapidly. It should only take a few seconds. Its purpose is to make you aware of your current experience and remember what has gone through your mind for the last couple of minutes. You are not to analyze your experience, you simply observe it.

The instructions are as follows:

- Focus your intention to be aware of your immediate experience.
- Ask yourself the question "How did I get here?"
- Attend to your immediate experience.

- Notice what other sensations, thoughts, or emotions come to mind.
- Trace those experiences over the last couple of minutes. Remember what you saw, felt, thought, or did over the last couple of minutes. Note what led to what during that time.
- Simply note the flow of your experiences over the last couple of minutes. Do *not* analyze where the experiences came from. This is especially important for people who have had experience with psychology. You are *not* psychoanalyzing yourself. All you are doing is observing the flow of your experience over the last couple of minutes.
- After a few seconds stop and reflect on what you have observed. Note any associations that seem important.

This exercise should be done several times per day. It is especially important to do this if you feel a sudden change in mood or body sensation.

After doing the brief attending exercise you may decide to take some action. Brian did a brief centering exercise to reduce the stress from the message he saw. He washed his face and got a glass of juice when he realized he was hungry. Maria decided to call her friend instead of ignoring their disagreement any longer.

BRIAN'S RESULTS FROM ATTENDING PRACTICE

Brian is sitting down for a meditation session to practice attending. He has been practicing attending while centering on the sensations of air moving in and out of his nose for about four weeks. It was difficult for him at first, but he is more comfortable with it now. He remembers his intention (his goals for meditation), and centers on the sensations of air moving in and out of his nose. He notes some tension in his shoulder, and disengages from it, moving his awareness back to the sensations in his nose. He then identifies the thought "You're tense today." He identifies this thought, and disengages from it. The thought returns, and he disengages from it again, going back to feeling the air moving in and out of his nose. The thought returns and Brian identifies his mind's activity as "thinking." This makes the thought "You're tense" seem more distant. He is able to disengage from it and go back to being aware of his nose. Then his mind settles down for a few breaths. Brian notes that the distractions are much easier to disengage from. He identifies even this as a thought, and goes back to being aware of his breath.

Brian continues to identify and disengage from distractions smoothly for the next few minutes. It takes effort, but is not straining him. Suddenly he remembers that he has a dentist appointment that afternoon. He identifies this thought, but when he tries to move his awareness back to the sensations in his nose, he can't quite feel them. Thoughts about his dental appointment seem to have grabbed his attention and won't let go. He tries to identify the thoughts, but there are too many and they are coming too fast. Brian realizes that he needs to try something else to disengage from these thoughts. He asks himself what his mind is doing, and labels the activity as "thinking." After telling himself that he is thinking a couple of times, he feels the intensity of the thoughts decrease. It feels like he has some distance from them. He is now able to disengage from them by moving his awareness back to his breath. He then identifies and disengages from several distractions in rapid succession: a feeling of anxiety, some tension in his neck, a thought about his neck being tense, some tension in his left shoulder, the feeling of anxiety. After another minute he is back to simply being calmly aware of the sensations of air flowing in and out of his nose.

Brian remembers some of the thoughts he was having about the dentist. He is tempted to analyze them to figure out why they might have been so intense. However, he remembers his teacher saying, **"As you practice attending, you may become fascinated by how thoughts, sensations, and emotions all flow from one into the other. Avoid analyzing them. Just continue to observe the flow during the practice. Any analysis should be done during the reflection stage of the session, or later in the day. The technique of attending is intended to train your ability to be aware and accepting of whatever your mind produces."** Brian identifies this thought, and goes back to being calmly aware of the sensations in his nose.

A few minutes later Brian's watch beeps at him, signaling the end of the session. As he reflects on his experience, he remembers the intense thoughts about the dentist, and realizes they were mostly about being in the dentist chair. He realizes that his discomfort comes from the experience of not being able to talk, not being able to say "Stop" when his dentist is causing him pain. He decides that he will set up a hand signal with his dentist that will mean "That hurts, stop, I want to say something to you." He feels a lot more comfortable about his upcoming appointment.

Brian also reflects on how attending is quite different from centering. It is a lot more work for him, but it yields a good deal more information. Attending seems to sharpen his mind. His mind moves more fluidly and more quickly as he identifies fleeting thoughts and sensations, and then disengages and goes back to centering on the sensations in his nose. He is also becoming aware of how sensations, thoughts, and emotions influence one another. Brian is looking forward to the next practice, *concentrating*.

MARIA'S RESULTS FROM ATTENDING PRACTICE

Maria is sitting for her afternoon meditation session after about four weeks of attending practice. She enjoys attending a lot, and has continued to practice even though she felt she could have gone on to the next practice a week ago. She remembers her intention and centers on the sensations of air moving in and out of her nose. Her mind is much calmer now than it used to be. There is a lot less mental noise. As thoughts come up and distract her, Maria identifies them quickly and goes back to her breath. She has the feeling that her mind is moving lightly from her breath to the distraction and then back to her breath. This sense of lightness is enjoyable. It keeps her from feeling caught by distressing thoughts. Along with it comes a feeling of smoother flow in her mind.

As Maria continues to sit, she is distracted by a distressing thought about a difficult situation at work. She identifies the thought, but it returns. Maria continues to center on her breath, and deliberately pays more attention to the sensations of air moving in and out of her nose. As she does this, she is again distracted by the thoughts about work. She identifies this activity as "thinking." She notes how the activity of thinking feels different from the activity of being aware of the sensations in her nose. Noticing this difference helps her to disengage from the thoughts about work. She is able to move her awareness back to the sensations of air moving in and out of her nose.

When her alarm chimes at the end of the session, Maria reflects on how she enjoys attending practice. It is much easier to identify distractions and disengage from them than to ignore them the way she tried to during centering practice. She had asked her teacher why she couldn't just have started with attending, and he responded, **"It is helpful to know how to center before you begin attending because you need to have a center to go back to. Otherwise you might not experience the back-and-forth movement of the mind. Your mind might just jump around from one thing to another, and that is not as helpful."**

Maria considers how this practice has reduced her feeling of being scattered. Instead of experiencing her mind jumping around like a Ping-Pong ball, she now feels that it moves more fluidly. It is like a flexible tree that can move freely but always comes back to its original position. Her mind is now receptive, and less reactive.

Maria has also learned that as she simply identifies thoughts, sensations, and emotions, over time they change and may even go away. As Maria identifies the distractions, she can easily separate out individual sensations and thoughts. She has a sense of how sometimes an emotion will distract her, and how that emotion is related to the thoughts going through her mind. Maria would like to continue to practice attending, but she remembers, **"You will find that certain practices are more enjoyable than others. That is because your mind's natural abilities fit with certain practices. Your natural flexibility and warmth make attending enjoyable. However, if you just practice what is easy for you, you will not develop the mental qualities you are lacking in. You need to move on to the next practice. You will continue to practice attending, but not in every session."**

Maria has been using the brief attending practice several times per day. She finds herself asking "How did I get here?" fairly spontaneously. She has gotten used to being surprised by the thoughts and images that arise when she does the practice. Many of them are bizarre and tend to be fearful and anxious. While they are somewhat based on reality, they are very unlikely to ever come about. She has learned to just accept these and avoid getting upset with them. She even has a sense of humor about this, a "There I go again" attitude. This keeps her on a more even keel throughout the day.

About three weeks after she began to practice attending, Maria discovered a way to use the practice to relax and help her get to sleep. One night, Maria was lying in bed and unable to sleep because of incessant thinking. She decided to just start paying attention to how her body was feeling. She lay still and centered on her breath while identifying and disengaging from the distracting thoughts. After a couple of minutes the thoughts began to slow down and become less bothersome. Maria then moved her awareness to her left foot. She centered on the sensations in her toes and foot while disengaging from the distracting thoughts. After a bit she moved her awareness up to her ankle. She felt how the toes, foot, and ankle were all connected, and how the sensations differed in each. If other thoughts entered her mind, she simply identified them and went back to focusing on the sensations. Maria continued to move her center of awareness upward until she was aware of her whole left leg. As she did this, her thoughts became fewer and quieter. She then repeated the process with her right leg. After that, she moved her awareness into her hips, pelvis, and then up into her abdomen. She hadn't quite finished being aware of her abdomen when she fell asleep.

When Maria asked her teacher about this, he was pleased. **"Good for you. You are playing around with the techniques and figuring out how to apply them. You centered on different areas of the body in turn while attending to sensations and thoughts. This can be very relaxing and, if done at bedtime, can often help you get to sleep. You can also use this as a relaxation exercise at other times."**

BRIAN AND MARIA are now both ready to move on to the next practice. Maria is more comfortable than Brian with the attending practice, because it uses her naturally strong mental qualities of flexibility and warmth. Both of them are experiencing benefits of increased insight and awareness. They are also more aware of constructive ideas and thoughts throughout the day. Their moods are generally more positive and they are more able to change their mental state when they are upset. They are more accepting of themselves and this helps them be more accepting of others.

REVIEW OF ATTENDING

Attending consists of identifying and disengaging from mental contents as they arise. The mental contents can be thoughts, sensations, emotions, or combinations of these. Each item is identified and then disengaged from. In the beginning stages, attending is combined with centering. The center acts as an anchor to keep the mind from drifting off. The basic attending technique is to center on the sensations of air moving in and out of your nose and attend to distractions. Anything that distracts you from being aware of your nose is identified and then disengaged from as you bring your attention back to your nose.

The disengagement process can take more effort than simply "letting go." Often the distractions have grabbed your mind, and letting go of them doesn't make them let go of you. Here are four ways of disengaging from distractions:

- Exert some effort and deliberately pay more attention to what you were centering on
- Identify the distractions quickly, before they have a chance to entangle you
- Tell the distraction, "Later!" after you have identified it
- Identify the mental activity that is associated with the distraction: sensing, thinking, or feeling

You are to practice the extended attending technique for periods of at least fifteen minutes for a total time of at least ninety minutes per week. You do not need to practice the extended centering practice anymore. A sign of success is when you experience your mind going easily back and forth between your center and the distractions.

Attending is like sitting on the bank of a river, watching what goes by. You want to identify what flows past as precisely as possible, without getting caught and pulled into the river. Sometimes objects on the river get caught in an eddy and take a while to move downstream. But eventually everything moves along. Another, more modern, analogy might be that attending is like visiting a web page where banner ads and pop-up ads appear. You identify these but you return your awareness to the web page without clicking on the ads.

You are ready to move on to the next practice when you can identify and disengage from distractions easily, without getting caught by them, for about two minutes.

The brief attending technique, called "How did I get here?" consists of checking in with what is going through your mind several times per day. Each time, you are to just observe the thoughts, sensations, and emotions that are on your mind without analyzing them. The period of observation should last up to thirty seconds, no more. This will help you be more aware of the background mental activity your mind is putting out during the day.

TIPS FOR THE PRACTICE OF ATTENDING

- Remember your intention at the start of each extended session by reviewing your intended results for meditation and the immediate purpose of the session, which is to identify and disengage from distractions while centering on the sensations of air moving in and out of your nose. Setting your intention takes only a couple of seconds, but increases the effectiveness of your practice.
- Before executing the brief practice, set your intention simply to be aware of what is on your mind.
- Alertness is very important in attending practice. Make sure you stay awake during the sessions. Washing your face with cold water or sitting in a more upright position can help.

- If you are feeling physical discomfort during a session and you cannot seem to disengage from it, then it is OK to move to relieve the discomfort as long as you first identify it precisely.
- If you are feeling mental strain during a session, especially when you are first starting to practice attending, then stop doing the attending practice and just center on the sensations in your lower abdomen. This will keep you from straining your mind.
- You can also use attending and centering to relax. Center on different body areas in turn as you identify and disengage from other sensations, thoughts, or emotions. It is OK to do this at bedtime to help you fall asleep.

4 concentrating: developing mental clarity

CONCENTRATING, the third meditative practice, develops mental clarity. The mental clarity you develop by practicing concentrating will complement the mental warmth you've developed by practicing attending. As your mental clarity increases, you mind will become better at analyzing. You will perceive details more precisely and think more clearly about complex issues. In addition to improving your analytical skills, concentrating also improves your memory.

Concentrating requires you to focus your awareness intensely on an object. As you focus on that object, other objects or phenomena recede from awareness and you perceive the object you are concentrating on in more detail. Eventually everything may fade from your awareness except the object you are concentrating on.

You can concentrate on singular physical objects or phenomena—a picture, a sound, or a sensation. You can also concentrate on a mental object, such as a memory, an imagined experience, or an abstract quality such as compassion. Generally you start by concentrating on a physical object and move as quickly as possible to concentrating on a mental object. Concentrating on a mental object develops mental clarity more effectively than concentrating on a physical object.

The basic concentrating technique involves the following steps:

- Observe a simple physical object so that you will be able to remember it. We recommend you start by looking at a key.
- Concentrate by focusing your awareness, or "zooming in" on the key, noticing as many details as possible.
- Close your eyes and allow the memory of the object to appear. Experience the image of the key in your mind.
- If you are not experiencing the image of the key, wait about a minute (five to ten breaths) to see if the image does appear. If it does not, then refresh your memory by concentrating on the object again—that is, open your eyes and look at the key.
- Repeat these steps for the rest of the session.

When you are beginning, you will probably spend most of your time concentrating on the physical object and not experience a clear image, or any image, when you close your eyes. That is OK—you are still developing your concentration ability by exploring the details of the physical object. The mental image usually develops with practice.

Some people, however, do not improve their ability to experience the mental image of the object. The image remains just as difficult to visualize after one week as when they started. These people should work with the memory of a sound by humming a note to themselves, and then allowing the memory of the sound to appear in their mind. Some people will be unable to make progress with the memory of a sound either. They should work with the memory of a movement by closing and opening their hand, and then allowing the memory of the movement to appear in their mind.

The fact that some people are unable to make progress at first by concentrating on the visual memory may relate to their preferred learning style. Some people are visual, some are auditory, and others are kinesthetic. A visual learner would learn a set of instructions best by seeing them. An auditory learner would learn the instructions best by listening to them. The kinesthetic learner would learn the instructions best by being taken through an activity using them. Since most people are visual learners, we first ask people to concentrate on a simple memorized image. If they have too much difficulty with that, then we have them work with a memorized sound or a memorized movement.

The only way to succeed at concentrating on a mental experience is to have patience with yourself. A sense of humor also helps. Many times your mind does everything but concentrate on the image. Finally you have a little success. The image appears. Then, just as you are feeling hopeful, the image changes or disappears. If you are patient and can laugh at the random things your mind does, you will be able to keep practicing. If you keep practicing, then you will improve, just as we did.

BRIAN'S FIRST EXPERIENCE WITH CONCENTRATING

Brian is beginning his morning meditation session, his first time practicing concentrating. He sits comfortably, remembers his intention, and looks at the key he has in his hand. It is an old house key from years ago. Brian holds the key flat in his palm and examines it. He notes its bronze color and its shape. He notes how the shape changes from one end of the key to the other. After examining the key for about a minute, he closes his eyes and waits for the image of the key to appear in his mind.

At first nothing happens. All he is aware of is a sort of reddish color with dark splotches. He assumes this is what his eyes are seeing of the back of his eyelids. He continues to wait expectantly. Suddenly he sees the image of the key. But when he concentrates on the image, all but the tip of the key disappears. Brian squints his closed eyes, looking inwardly to see where the other part of the key went. That causes the tip of the key to disappear too. Brian strains harder trying to see the key. He then remembers, **"Resist the temptation to use your eyes to look for the mental image of the key. Just let the image appear in your mind. Your eyes should feel totally relaxed. It is normal for the image to come and go, or to appear in bits and pieces. If you lose track of the image, just open your eyes and refresh your memory."**

The image of the key is completely gone, so Brian opens his eyes and looks at the key again. After a few seconds, he closes his eyes and waits for the image to appear in his mind. This time it comes quickly, but it is pointing in a different position. Brian tries to rotate the image in his mind and feels like he is straining his neck. **"Accept the image your mind produces and concentrate on it. Do not try to manipulate it at this early stage. If the position changes, just observe the details clearly."**

Brian begins to realize that concentration is different from control. He opens his eyes again and looks at the key. Then he closes his eyes and waits for the image to appear in his mind. Again he gets bits and pieces of it. Suddenly he perceives the whole key as if he were looking at it. Then, just as he realizes that, the image fades. The exercise is frustrating him. **"It can be very difficult to stabilize a mental image, even a simple one. In fact, if you can maintain the image of the key for more than a couple of seconds at a time, you are doing well. In order to succeed at concentrating, be patient with yourself**

and refresh your memory by opening your eyes and looking at the key in your hand frequently. It is OK to do that every minute if you need to."

Brian allows himself a mental groan and opens his eyes again to look at the key. This time when he closes them, he finds a partial image of the key appears quickly. Instead of trying to make the rest of the key appear, he just concentrates on the part that has appeared. He notes with surprise that there are a couple of details that he was not aware of seeing on the key in his hand. He opens his eyes to check on this and realizes that the image in his mind was correct. Pleased, he closes his eyes again.

Images of bits and pieces of the key appear and disappear for the rest of Brian's meditation session. When his alarm goes off, he feels a sense of relief, and reflects on how difficult this seemingly simple exercise is. He also realizes that it is a lot easier if he accepts the difficulty and opens his eyes to look at the key frequently. He decides that he should take the advice of his teacher by accepting what happens and trusting that he will improve over time.

MARIA'S FIRST EXPERIENCE WITH CONCENTRATING

Maria is beginning her first session of concentration. She remembers her intention and then looks at her car key, which she is holding in front of her. She examines the flat side of the key, noting as many details as she can. As she notices more and more details, she wonders how she will ever remember them all and starts to feel overwhelmed. **"You do not need to consciously memorize all the details of the object. Your mind is aware of them and will recall them for you with practice."**

Maria then closes her eyes and waits for the image of the key to appear in her mind. After a bit, her mind becomes noisy with random thoughts. She identifies these as thoughts and goes back to waiting for the image of the key to appear. She realizes that she has forgotten what it looked like. This is irritating and she notes her mind scolding her. She remembers her teacher's words: **"Be gentle with yourself. If you lose track of the mental image of the key, the solution is to open your eyes and refresh your memory. Getting upset or scolding yourself will just slow you down. So when you have difficulty, simply open your eyes and refresh your memory."**

Maria opens her eyes, looks at the key again for a few seconds, and closes her eyes. After a bit, the outline of the key has appeared. It seems to be somewhere above her head. She wonders if it should be in front of her, but it doesn't seem to want to move. **"The image is to appear in your mind. Since you are not using your eyes, the image may seem to appear anywhere at first. Common places are in front of your eyes, inside your head, or above your head. Don't worry about where the image appears, just observe the details."**

Maria looks at the outline, but no other details appear. She opens her eyes again to refresh her memory. This time, after she closes her eyes, she perceives the image of the key in front of her. However, it is rotating slowly in a counterclockwise direction. When she tries to stop the rotation, it begins to rotate about its long axis, showing her first an edge and then a flat side in turn. **"Just observe the details of the image that appears in your mind. Do not try to force the image in your mind to behave in any particular way."** Maria watches the key rotate and then it fades away.

Maria refreshes her memory again, closes her eyes, and finds herself looking at the image of the family's pet cat. The image is quite clear and seems as if the cat is in front of her. She waits, but no image of the key appears. The cat suddenly changes into a lamp, which then fades. Maria wonders if there is something wrong with her; the images seem a little bizarre. **"When you wait for the image of the key to appear in your mind, sometimes your mind produces other images. Just observe them, and continue to wait for the image of the key to appear. If you just identify the images and disengage**

from them without getting emotionally caught up with them, then eventually they will disappear. If the image of the key does not appear, then open your eyes and refresh your memory of it." Maria smiles at herself, opens her eyes, looks at the key for a few seconds, and then closes her eyes again.

Maria continues to perceive random images throughout the rest of the session. Occasionally she gets a glimpse of the image of the key. But those moments are rare. She is able to stay relaxed and simply identify and disengage from the other images. When her alarm goes off, she reflects on how her mind did seem to generate complete images, but it had a great deal of difficulty keeping the images still or producing the image she wanted to concentrate upon. When she feels frustrated with this, she remembers, **"You can be pleased that your mind is producing images, even if they are not the images you want. The ability of your mind to produce images at all is useful."** Maria lets out a sigh, reminds herself that patience is a virtue, reorients to her body, time, and place, and then opens her eyes.

PRINCIPLES OF CONCENTRATING

Concentrating involves focusing your awareness on an object and perceiving it in complete detail. The object you focus on can be physical, such as a key or a picture, or it can be a sound. You can also focus on nonphysical objects, such as a memory, an imagined experience, or an abstract concept. As your strength of concentration increases, you will perceive more details about the object, and experience fewer distractions.

When you start to practice concentrating, we advise you to focus on a physical object and then the memory of that object. The object should also be emotionally neutral, not something you feel very strongly about. Brian and Maria are beginning with concentrating on a key. A key is a small familiar object with enough detail to be challenging but not overwhelming.

Concentrating on a mental experience can be extremely difficult, especially at first. There are numerous difficulties that can arise. Brian is experiencing the difficulty of seeing only one piece of the image at a time. He is able to see a part clearly, but his mind does not see the whole image. Maria has the difficulty of seeing other images than the one she wants to concentrate upon. Fortunately these difficulties decrease with practice. Patience is very necessary. Just refreshing your memory by looking at the key again is the best way to deal with the difficulties. Your mind may have a great deal of difficulty stabilizing mental images at first, but it rapidly improves with practice.

INSTRUCTIONS FOR THE EXTENDED CONCENTRATING TECHNIQUE

- Sit in a comfortable place where you are not likely to be disturbed. Quiet is important, so find a setting with as few distractions as possible.
- Remember your intention by thinking about your long-range goals for meditation, and your immediate goal for the session. Your immediate goal for this exercise is to concentrate on a key and then the memory of that key.
- Hold the key in your hand so that one of the flat sides is facing you. Concentrate on the key by gazing at it gently, observing the details of its shape, color, and any distinctive markings. Spend about a minute doing this.
- Then close your eyes and remember the key, allowing the image to appear in your mind. It is very important to have the sense of allowing the image to appear. There should be no sense of straining your eyes or squinting to see something.

- If other images appear or if distracting thoughts arise, simply identify them and go back to waiting for the image of the key to appear.
- If the image of the key does not appear after a minute or so, then simply open your eyes, concentrate on the key in your hand for a few seconds, and then close your eyes again.
- If the image of the key or a part of the key appears when you have your eyes closed, concentrate on the details of the image. When the image fades or if the image stays incomplete, then open your eyes again and concentrate on the key.
- It is better to stay relaxed and have to open your eyes frequently than to strain or force the image to appear.
- Continue to repeat the process of looking at the key and then closing your eyes and waiting for its image to appear in your mind.

Patience is very important in this practice. If you have the whole image appear in your mind and can observe the details for even one or two seconds, you are doing well. Most people have to look at the key about every minute on the average when they start practicing. That is OK. By accepting what you can do you will make faster progress than if you try to force your mind to do what it cannot. Just keep opening your eyes to refresh your memory and then closing them again.

The extended concentration technique just described is to be done in sessions of about fifteen minutes.

BRIEF CONCENTRATING PRACTICE: "WHAT HAPPENED THEN?"

There is also a brief concentration technique that you need to practice as well. The purpose of the brief exercise is to train your mind to focus intensely and quickly on something that is not physically present. This brief practice will dramatically improve your ability to concentrate. It will improve your memory and the clarity of your thinking as well.

To do the brief practice, you are to spend one or two minutes remembering an emotionally neutral event from earlier in the day. You should remember as many details from the event as possible. The details can be from more than one sense; you can remember sights, sounds, smells, sensations, and movements.

BRIAN'S EXPERIENCE WITH THE BRIEF CONCENTRATING PRACTICE

Brian is sitting down in his living room on a Saturday afternoon. He has nothing particular to do and is enjoying being relaxed. He remembers that he needs to practice brief concentration by concentrating on the details of an emotionally neutral event from earlier in the day. He closes his eyes and tries to remember breakfast that morning.

At first he is surprised to find that he doesn't recall having breakfast. He knows he ate breakfast, but the memory is not coming to him. He knows he ate cereal this morning, and with that thought he remembers sitting down at the table with a bowl of cereal. He observes the details of the memory, the look of the cereal in the bowl, the feel of the bowl and the spoon in his hand, the smell and taste of the cereal, and his body posture as he ate. He sees his son coming in and sitting down at the table and hears himself greet him. Some of the details are less clear than others, but Brian just observes what he can.

After a couple of minutes concentrating on breakfast, Brian reflects on the experience. He realizes that some of the details were clear, but other details, especially things in his peripheral vision, were not. He also realizes that he sounded rather gruff when he greeted his son. He did not feel upset with him and decides that he should work on speaking in a more gentle tone of voice. Brian yawns, stretches, and opens his eyes. The whole brief technique has taken about two minutes.

MARIA'S EXPERIENCE WITH THE BRIEF CONCENTRATING PRACTICE

Maria is sitting at her desk at work when she remembers that she is to be practicing brief concentration. She doesn't particularly like the extended concentration exercises and wonders if the brief practice is all that necessary. **"Concentration can be one of the most frustrating exercises for some people. It is also vital if you are to develop all your mental qualities. The brief exercises will help you immensely."**

Maria remembers her intention to recall an event from earlier in the day. She closes her eyes and tries to remember breakfast. Nothing appears in her mind. She knows she ate breakfast, but she simply cannot recall doing so. Suddenly she has the clear image of brushing her teeth before leaving for work. She can see herself putting the toothpaste on the toothbrush, feel the movement of putting the brush in her mouth, taste and smell the toothpaste, and even see her reflection in the mirror. She is pleased by the clarity of the memory, but wonders if she has done the practice correctly since it was not the memory she planned on. **"When doing the brief practice, it is the clarity of the details that is important. If you**

access a memory that is different from the one you planned, that is OK. You will gain more accuracy over time." Maria reflects on her mind's ability to perceive details in mental images. It just seems to have its own ideas about what images to perceive. She reminds herself to have patience. She then stretches her arms, wiggles her toes, and opens her eyes.

One evening Maria wants to go to the store to get some milk. She looks in her purse but cannot find her car keys there. She realizes she can't recall where she put them and starts to feel frustrated. "I'm always losing my car keys!" she thinks to herself. Then she decides to try using the brief concentrating practice to find her keys. She remembers her intention to recall what she did with her car keys. She then closes her eyes and thinks about the last time she knew she had her keys. She knew she had them when she drove home from work. She sees herself take them out of the ignition and feels herself holding them in her hand as she walks into the house. She then sees her daughter run up and give her a hug. She drops her purse but keeps hold of the keys while she hugs her daughter. Then the phone rings and she puts down her daughter and drops the keys on the counter while she answers the phone. The call is for her husband. She remembers writing a message for him on a sheet of paper and putting it on the counter. Then she watches herself pick up her purse and put it away; however, she does not see herself pick up her keys after she put them on the counter. Maria opens her eyes and walks over to the counter. Her keys are not in view. She lifts up the sheet of paper on which she wrote the message to her husband. Under it she sees her car keys. Maria laughs and feels pleased by her success.

INSTRUCTIONS FOR THE BRIEF CONCENTRATING PRACTICE: "WHAT HAPPENED THEN?"

We call the brief concentrating technique "What Happened Then?" It involves spending a couple of minutes remembering an emotionally neutral event from earlier in the day. It is better that the event be emotionally neutral because that permits your mind to perceive details clearly without getting caught up in emotional turmoil.

The instructions are as follows:

- Remember your intention to recall an emotionally neutral event from earlier in the day.
- Close your eyes and remember the event. Notice as many sensory details as you can. These include sight, hearing, smell, taste, touch, and kinesthetic sensations.
- If nothing comes to mind, then prime your mind by thinking about the event. While you think about the event, be alert for any imagined experiences that arise.
- Allow these to appear in your mind, and observe the details. After one or two minutes reflect on what you experienced and open your eyes.
- If a different event comes to mind than the one you wanted, accept that and observe the details.
- As you get better at this technique, you can practice it with your eyes open. You can also practice remembering more emotionally intense experiences.

BRIAN'S RESULTS FROM CONCENTRATING PRACTICE

Brian is beginning a meditation session after six weeks of practicing concentration. The technique has become easier for him, and he feels relaxed as he remembers his intention. He remembers his goals for meditation, and his goal of using this session to concentrate on the mental image of the key. Brian opens his eyes briefly to glance at the key and refresh his memory of its shape. He has become so familiar with it that this takes only a couple of seconds. As he closes his eyes, he experiences a brief darkness, and then sees the image of the key as if it was floating in front of his face. The image appears quite clear and steady. He is vaguely aware of some thoughts in the back of his mind, but they do not seem to be distracting him. The image of the key seems to be getting brighter, and the details even sharper. Brian also begins to have the impression that he can perceive more than just visual details about the key. He can feel the smoothness of its surface, and he even has a sense of its weight and hardness. His mind moves along the key from the tip to the back, noticing each bump and ridge. Even as his awareness zooms in on the tiny details, Brian keeps an awareness of the whole key.

The experience is fascinating. Brian feels a sense of mental clarity, as if there is almost nothing separating him from the key. Suddenly he realizes that he has lost track of his surroundings and indeed has no idea if he is even breathing. This jolts him a bit, and he becomes aware of his body sitting comfortably and breathing easily. Brian has lost track of time, and he wonders if his alarm went off without him hearing it. He struggles with this thought and then just opens his eyes and checks his watch. He is astonished to find that only three minutes have passed, because it felt like it could have been hours. **"When your mind gets absorbed in concentration, it does not keep**

track of time. The experience is timeless. After you come out of concentration, your mind comes up with some estimate as to the amount of time that has passed. This estimate can be wrong, but just observe it and let it go. You also do not have to worry about concentrating and missing your alarm. Since you have been using the alarm to alert you to the end of a session for a couple of months, your mind has been trained to recognize it and inform you, even if you do not notice it consciously."

Brian is excited and pleased by the experience. He closes his eyes again, expecting to have the key appear in the same kind of detail. However, this time nothing happens. He wonders what is wrong and feels the beginnings of frustration. As he observes what is going on, he realizes that his excitement had jarred his body a little, so it is no longer as relaxed. **"Concentration is easier when the body is relaxed. If you are excited, or agitated, then just center on your abdomen or do some other relaxing meditation until you settle down. Then go back to concentrating."**

Brian decides to use the brief centering practice, which he finds quite relaxing. He thinks "Calm" as he breathes in and "Relaxed" as he breathes out. After a couple of minutes, he feels himself settle and his muscles loosen. Brian then recalls the image of the key from his memory, and within a short time it appears again. His experience is not as detailed or absorbing this time, but he is able to hold the image steady. After a few seconds, the image fades, but he is able to recall it without opening his eyes. **"The experience of concentration is variable, especially in the beginning. Sometimes your concentration is intense and you are absorbed in the experience, and other times the mental images are more fleeting and ephemeral. Just accept the variability and enjoy the experience you do have."** Brian continues to have the key appear and reappear in his mind for the rest of the session. As he reflects on his experience, he notices that his mind feels curiously rested and invigorated. This is a pleasant sensation and he rises from his sitting posture with a bounce in his step and a smile on his face.

Over the last six weeks, Brian has noticed benefits from concentrating practice. His thinking is clearer at work, and the brief practice has helped him remember details from meetings and take better notes. This has improved his efficiency at work and lowered his stress. Brian is also finding that he can focus more intently on his golf game. He is much more aware of details in his swing, and he is finding things to correct that he used to be unaware of. The brief practice has also made him aware of how gruff he sounds around the house, and he is changing that by consciously speaking in a softer, warmer voice. Brian has also noticed some of the negative nonverbal cues he gives when he is upset at work. One of these is clenching his fist when he is talking with a subordinate. He is working on keeping his hand open when he talks, and this is helping him to stay calmer.

Brian has also used the concentration practice to help himself relax before going to sleep. He discovered that he could imagine scenes from some vacations he had taken that were quite enjoyable. He found that imagining these scenes was quite peaceful. One night when he was restless and could not get to sleep, he began to imagine a scene from when he had gone camping. As he concentrated on the scene, he found himself settling down and getting lost in it. Soon he felt like he was dreaming and then he remembered waking up in the morning. He asked his teacher about this. **"Concentration practice will improve your ability to visualize. You have discovered a way to use the skill of visualization to help you sleep. We will be using your increased ability to visualize as we work on applications of meditation."**

MARIA'S RESULTS FROM CONCENTRATING PRACTICE

Maria has been practicing concentration for several weeks. It has been difficult, for she continued to have a lot of trouble seeing the key in her mind. Bits and pieces of it would appear, but then they would rapidly fade, and she continued to get lots of distracting images. After a week without any progress, she felt like she was straining very hard and getting nowhere. Her concentration sessions were becoming exhausting, and she couldn't seem to help but strain her eyes in order to try to see the key more clearly. Maria got her teacher's advice: **"Some people have a difficult time seeing things in their mind because they are not visual. These people do better concentrating on the memory of a sound or a movement. Practice concentrating on the memory of a sound. Hum a note and let the memory of the sound appear in your mind. If the sound does not appear in your mind, then refresh your memory by humming the note again."**

Maria tried this and found it somewhat easier. However, it was still somewhat exhausting. Her teacher next suggested that she work with a kinesthetic memory. **"Sit comfortably and then close and open your right hand. Do that several times, paying attention to the sense of movement. Notice how the sensations in your fingers and the rest of your hand changes as you close and open your right hand. After doing that several times, keep your hand still and allow the memory of the movement to appear in your mind."** She found that easier. Her mind seemed to be able to perceive and remember the kinesthetic sensations more easily than the sound of the note or the sight of the key.

Maria is now sitting down for an extended session of concentration. It has been about eight weeks since she started practicing concentration, and about four weeks since she started practicing concentrating on kinesthetic sensations. Maria remembers her intention for the session, and allows herself to breathe easily for a few minutes to settle down. Maria then closes and opens her right hand very slowly several times. As she closes the hand, she notes the tactile sensations as her fingers flex. She notes the sensations inside her hand, focusing on them more than external sensations. After doing this several times, she leaves her hand open and then remembers what it felt like to close and open her hand. Her mind seems very peaceful today, and suddenly she has the sense that her hand is actually opening and closing. The feeling is somewhat odd because she can't quite seem to figure out where the feeling is. She is aware of her physical hand lying open in her lap, however she can also feel the same hand opening and closing. Maria focuses more intently on the imagined sensations of movement in her hand, and as she does so, the awareness of her physical hand disappears.

Maria begins to feel a sense of warmth in this "imaginary" hand, and a sense of deep comfort. Time seems to slow down as she observes the imagined kinesthetic sensations of movement in her hand. The hand seems to be opening and closing in incredibly slow motion. Maria's awareness is absorbed by the sensations of movement and her experience. She feels a very pleasant connection with this imaginary hand. Maria suddenly realizes that she has gotten lost in the exercise and has completely lost track of time, the rest of her body, and her surroundings. This realization startles her and she goes through a brief period of disorientation as she connects to the rest of her body. For a little bit, she has a sensation that she has two right hands; the imaginary one feels stronger than the real one. As she pays attention to her body, the imaginary one fades by joining with the actual right hand. Maria notices, as she opens and closes her actual right hand, that she now seems much more aware of the kinesthetic perceptions that occur during those movements. She is aware of enjoying the movement more than she ever had before. As Maria is doing this, she suddenly hears her watch alarm go off. She's amazed that the time is up and realizes that over twenty minutes had gone by while she was absorbed in concentrating on the memory of her hand moving.

Maria reflects on this experience. She notes how kinesthetic perceptions are much easier for her to concentrate on than auditory or visual images. She also notes how this deep concentration is giving her a new appreciation for her body. She feels more comfortable inside it. Maria takes some time to bring her awareness to the rest of her body. She then reorients to time and place in a gradual manner, making sure she remembers her surroundings before she wiggles her fingers and toes and opens her eyes. **"After getting absorbed in an experience of concentration it is important to return to the waking state in a gentle manner. Of course, if you had to respond to an emergency, you would be able to do so quickly. However, if you have the time, it is more gentle for you to change states in a gradual manner. So, take some time to bring your awareness to the rest of your body, remember the day and the time, remember the place and your surroundings, and then wiggle your fingers and toes and take some deep breaths before you open your eyes."**

In spite of the difficulty she has had with concentrating, Maria is experiencing a number of benefits. She is thinking more clearly, and this helps her think through the details of complex situations more easily. She also has an increased awareness of her body's sensations. Often, when under stress, she would move quickly and somewhat erratically. Now, she is able to move more slowly and more smoothly, which seems to keep her mental state calmer. Maria's husband has commented on how she seems less upset when under pressure. Her memory for small tasks that she needs to accomplish during the day has improved. She is also able to remember ideas for work that happened to occur at random times. In the past she would often forget these ideas before she had a chance to write them down. Now she is able to remember them.

REVIEW OF CONCENTRATING

Concentrating consists of focusing attention on an object with such intensity that all the details of the object are perceived clearly. The intensity of the focus can be so great that you may lose track of the outside world (everything except the object). When beginning to learn concentrating, you concentrate on a physical object and the memory of that object. Brian and Maria both started off with concentrating on the memorized image of a key. If a visual memory is too difficult to use, then you can use the memory of a simple sound, or a simple movement, as Maria did.

We recommend that you practice concentration in this way for at least fifteen minutes at a time for a total of sixty minutes per week. In addition, you should spend at least thirty minutes per week practicing attending.

Avoid straining in order to perceive the mental image. You are to just allow the memory to appear in your mind and refresh your memory with the object if the memory fades.

You are ready to move on when you can concentrate on the memory of the object and hold it steady for about ten seconds.

The brief concentration technique, called "What Happened Then?" consists of remembering the details of an event from earlier in the day. You are to spend up to two minutes remembering. As you concentrate on the memory of the event, use as many senses as possible: sight, touch, hearing, smell, taste, and kinesthetic.

The combination of the brief and extended practice sessions will improve your ability to concentrate. You will also find that your memory improves, and that your ability to think about abstract concepts increases.

TIPS FOR THE PRACTICE OF CONCENTRATING

- Remember your intention at the start of each session, and reflect on what happened in each session as you finish.
- If you are not able to recall the visual image when you first start, make sure you are using a simple enough image. Working with the image of a key seems to be good for most people. Some people may need to start with something simpler, such as the image of a number, letter, or simple symbol.
- If you can't remember visual images at all, then use the memory of a simple sound or hand movement to concentrate on.
- Patience is the most important virtue when learning concentration. When you first start, just remind yourself that it doesn't matter how often you have to refresh your memory by looking at the object.
- It is very important to avoid any sense of straining your eyes to make the image appear in your mind. If you feel any strain in your eyes, then open them and look at the object in order to refresh your memory.
- As you finish the session, reflect on your experience, and then reorient gradually to your surroundings.

5 opening: experiencing spaciousness, the key to your creativity

OPENING develops the mental quality of spaciousness. Spaciousness is the mental quality that complements the other four: steadiness, flexibility, warmth, and clarity. Spaciousness is the key to creativity. It enables us to organize our perceptions, thoughts, and other mental objects into completely new patterns. Opening techniques help our minds experience spaciousness directly so that we become familiar with that quality. As we learn to open and experience spaciousness, we learn to change our perceptions and conceptualizations about ourselves and the world we experience.

Our mind organizes its perceptions into a familiar experience we call reality. However, that familiar experience is only one of many possible experiences of reality. Opening helps us to let go of one particular way of experiencing reality so that we can experience something else. The experience of letting go is the experience of spaciousness. Once we have let go, then our mind can create something else out of the spaciousness.

Another simple example of this occurs when we look at a cube drawn on paper. Even though the shape is two-dimensional, our mind sees one of two possible three-dimensional cubes. When we see one of the cubes, our mind is holding on to a familiar experience of reality. When we see the other cube, our mind is holding on to a different experience of reality. What occurs when we make the transition from seeing one cube to seeing the other is the process of opening and the experience of spaciousness.

As you cultivate spaciousness, you will find that

- You will have more creative ideas
- You will be better at finding solutions for problems that you have been stuck on
- You will see different perspectives to a situation
- You will find yourself laughing more
- You will realize how much of what you worry about doesn't really matter

Spaciousness can lead to leaps of intuition that free the mind from traps caused by excessive thinking. This is illustrated by the following story:

When I, Lobsang, was training at the Buddhist School of Dialectics in Dharamsala, I studied Buddhist teachings from five o'clock in the morning until about 11:30 at night. I did this every day and became so engrossed in the pursuit of philosophical knowledge that it was my only activity for months. Nearly every moment of my time was spent learning how to think, analyze, debate, and in memorizing more philosophical ideas.

One day I took the afternoon off and walked to the waterfalls that cascaded down the mountains about a mile from the monastery. I was alone, and I sat in the stillness in which the only sound was the rushing of the waterfall. As I watched, I became aware of the continuity between the changes I could see in the flow of the water and the variations in the sound. Soon the continuity between the flow of the water and the sound of the water appeared constant and unchanging.

Suddenly, my mind leaped to a new perspective. I realized the sound and the flow of the water were not constant, but endlessly changing. My mind leaped again and I realized that my thoughts, as well as the ideas and theories I had been grasping, were also changing and impermanent. I reflected that without this sudden burst of spaciousness, despite so steadfastly studying Buddhism, I would have missed the very essence of its teaching, centering as it does on impermanence and openness.

Opening techniques that cultivate spaciousness are quite easy for most people to learn, once they have practiced attending and concentrating with some dedication. When you start to practice opening, you should continue to practice attending and concentrating in some of the extended sessions. Do only one technique during each extended session. We recommend that you divide the extended sessions equally among the three techniques: attending, concentrating, and opening. For example, if you are doing three thirty-minute sessions per week, like Maria, then you would do one session each of attending, concentrating, and opening per week.

Opening techniques require us to disengage from our usual way of experiencing reality. One way to do this is to vividly remember a time when you experienced a sense of space or vastness. We usually keep a tight grip on the orientation of our body as the localized origin of our experience. When we concentrate on the experience of vastness, we can experience a loosening of that grip as well as a shift to a more nonlocal experience. This shift is the result of experiencing spaciousness.

The other type of technique we will be teaching is to become aware of a body experience that is somewhat ambiguous. By attending to the ambiguity and allowing our mind to accept the confusion about our body experience we can facilitate a shift of that experience.

BRIAN'S FIRST EXPERIENCE WITH SPACIOUSNESS: "OUTER SPACE"

Brian is beginning his morning meditation session. He is starting to practice opening today and on the advice of his teacher he has gotten up a little earlier. **"Opening techniques tend to change your state of consciousness in a more powerful way than the other practices. You want to allow enough time to make the shift in your state of consciousness and return to your usual one before the end of the session. Fifteen minutes is not really enough time to do that. A better minimum is twenty minutes."**

Brian is now used to waking early and he enjoys his meditation sessions, so getting up five minutes earlier is acceptable. He sits down on the pillow in his living room and remembers his intention for the session. He recalls his goals and thinks briefly about the purpose of this session: experiencing a sense of mental vastness and a letting go. He notices that he feels a little tense, especially in his shoulders and neck. **"If you feel tense, then spend a little time getting relaxed so you will be better able to perform the technique. Centering on the sensations in the lower abdomen as you breathe is a good way to get the mind and body into a calm state from which you can start other practices."** Brian centers on the sensations in his lower abdomen for a couple of minutes. As he feels the warmth in his lower abdomen he relaxes, and the muscles in his shoulders and neck loosen.

Brian now feels ready to do the opening technique. He remembers times when he was in a place where he felt a sense of vastness, of space all around him. One memory is of a time when he was on a mountaintop. Another was when he was at the seashore looking out over the ocean. In both experiences, he was alone and he remembers the sense of being able to see forever. As he becomes more aware of these memories, the one of the mountaintop seems to have a greater sense of the vastness to it. Brian focuses on that, and the memory of the seashore fades.

Brian concentrates on the details of the mountaintop experience that give him that sense of vastness. He notices the feel of the air, the blue of the sky, the ground falling away beneath him, and the expanse of land stretching out to the horizon in all directions. As he focuses on these details, he suddenly has the sense that he is not remembering correctly. He feels as if his body is much larger in the memory than it should be. He feels a little jolt of surprise as he realizes this. The memory vanishes suddenly and he is back sitting on his pillow with his eyes closed. He remembers that his teacher said, **"When we do the opening techniques, a sign of success is that our experience of how we perceive our bodies changes. The spaciousness occurs when we have let go of how we usually experience our selves. That allows a different experience to move in. If this new experience seems unusual, our mind may get a little startled and move back to the experience we are used to. Just accept this, realize that the technique was successful, and continue practicing it."**

Brian is pleased with himself. It was exciting to experience himself as a huge being on top of a mountain. He refocuses his mind on the memory of being on the mountaintop again. He tries to remember what it felt like to experience himself as being huge. However, his mind does not seem to want to cooperate. He notices the details of the mountaintop, but his body continues to feel like it usually does.

He starts to get frustrated. **"When you experience a sensory alteration while practicing opening, there is a temptation to try to evoke the same altered sensations the next time you practice. This is a mistake. You need to do the opening technique and let go of trying to evoke any particular change. When your mind experiences the spaciousness, the changes will come and you simply allow them to flow as they arise and dissolve."**

Brian remembers this advice and realizes that he needs to refocus on the sense of vastness. That in itself is enjoyable, even without the sensory changes. Brian remembers how peaceful it was to look out from the mountaintop and see the land stretching out beneath him. He was aware of the sights below him, but they were all at a distance and he could encompass them all in his vision. As Brian gets absorbed in this experience of vastness, he suddenly realizes that he does not know where he is. He has a moment of complete uncertainty and then feels as if he is floating above the mountaintop and moving higher into the sky. As he starts to think about this, the sensation fades and he is back to being aware of remembering the mountaintop while he sits on his pillow in his living room. **"The experience of not knowing where you are, the uncertainty, is a sign of spaciousness. In that spaciousness your mind is not grasping on to anything, it has let go. When it has opened like that, it can then create an experience that may be quite different from your usual way of experiencing things."**

Brian feels a little tired and finds himself just centering on the sensations in his lower abdomen. Suddenly he hears his alarm beep at him. He is surprised the session is over already. He reflects on the sense of vastness that he experienced and also the change in his time perception. He then brings his awareness back to his whole body, reorients himself to time and place, and then opens his eyes.

MARIA'S FIRST EXPERIENCE WITH SPACIOUSNESS: "INNER SPACE"

Maria sits down for her first session of opening. She remembers her intention, recalling her goals for meditation and this session, and closes her eyes. Maria centers her awareness on the sensations of air moving in and out of her nose. She attends to thoughts and sensations as they arise, identifying and disengaging from them. After a couple of minutes, she feels her mind and body settle into a comfortable, relaxed state. Now that she is relaxed, she is ready to do the opening technique.

Maria brings her attention to the sensations of movement in her chest as she breathes, how her chest expands and contracts. She observes how the movement occurs in her back and sides as well as the front. She focuses her attention more and more on the movement of her chest and less on the movement of the air. As Maria becomes more aware of the expansion and contraction of her chest, she also starts to notice some movement in her abdomen. She notices that her abdomen expands and contracts, too. She becomes aware that her shoulders lift slightly as she inhales and fall slightly as she exhales. As she observes the sensations of expansion and contraction, Maria notices that she cannot be quite sure where the expansion and contraction begin and end. She can feel her chest expanding and contracting, but she is not sure how far that movement extends into her shoulders. She can feel her abdomen expanding and contracting, but she is not quite sure how far that movement extends down into her pelvis and hips.

Maria accepts the uncertainty and then begins to imagine that other parts of her body are expanding and contracting as well. As she focuses on the expansion in her chest and the lift of her shoulders, she imagines that her neck and upper arms are expanding as well. She then feels as if her neck and upper arms contract as her shoulders fall and her chest contracts. Then, as she feels her abdomen expand and contract, she imagines that her pelvic and hip area is expanding and contracting as well. Maria then allows the imagined sensations of expansion and contraction to move outward to her arms, hands, and legs.

She suddenly has the thought, "This is ridiculous. Your hands and feet can't be expanding and contracting!" But, she remembers, **"When you practice opening, you will be letting go of your usual way of experiencing things. That means you will be experiencing things that 'can't happen.' Just enjoy that and keep going along with your experience. Pretend 'as if' the changes were occurring."** Maria goes back to sensing the expansion and contraction in her chest, shoulders, and abdomen. After a few breaths, she imagines the expansion and contraction moving outward again, and soon feels as if her arms and legs are expanding and contracting as well.

Maria is feeling very quiet and peaceful. Soon she realizes that she has lost track of the usual size and shape of her body. She feels like a round ball, and then like an oval. She feels like she has become very large and then feels as if she is very small. Her thoughts seem to be at a great distance. They are quiet, lost in a sense of interior vastness. Even her sense of having a body begins to fade. Concepts of size and shape no longer seem to apply. Images come and go, but she does not notice them. She is just aware of a deep sense of peace and quiet, and feels like her awareness is floating in a sea of comfort.

Maria hears her watch alarm going off as if from a great distance. She reflects on how much her perceptions changed during this session. She also reflects on how varied her experience during opening meditation has been. **"It is normal to have a lot of variation in your experience when you practice opening. Some days nothing seems to happen, other days you have a lot of imagery, and others you have a radically altered experience of your body. Just accept the experience your mind gives you, and realize that any change in your perception was the result of an experience of spaciousness to some degree."** Maria feels a sense of gratitude for the experience. She then brings her attention to her whole body, wiggling her fingers and toes to restore her sense of her usual body's boundaries. She finds this takes a minute or so. She then remembers the day and time and her surroundings, gradually bringing her mind back to her current situation. After another minute she opens her eyes.

Maria still feels a little spacey, and fumbles a bit as she gets up from her session. She feels a little unsteady as she walks, almost as if she is not quite aware of where the floor is. **"When you first experience a deep sense of spaciousness, you may feel like you are not quite back to this reality after your meditation. If that is the case, have a light snack or wash your face in cold water and that will bring you back into your body."** Maria goes into the kitchen and makes herself a piece of toast. As she eats it, she feels like she is reorienting fully to her surroundings.

PRINCIPLES OF OPENING

Opening involves allowing your mind to experience a sense of vastness or spaciousness. When your mind becomes spacious, your usual way of perceiving reality is able to change.

People often respond differently to opening techniques, especially at first. We will give instructions for two different opening techniques. Pick one that feels good to you, and if it doesn't work try the other one.

Notice that the opening techniques used by Brian and Maria required some skill with concentrating and attending. Brian started by concentrating on an image and focusing on a particular aspect of the image: the vastness. Maria started by attending to sensations and then concentrating on a particular imagined sensory experience. Both of them used attending to identify and disengage from thoughts that were distracting them from the opening experience.

The experience of spaciousness occurs when your mind lets go of its usual way of organizing reality. Your mind then has the possibility of reorganizing reality in a different manner. When that happens, your perceptions change. The changes in your perceptions are the result of the spaciousness. They are not the actual experience of spaciousness. That is why the particular changes are not important. If your perceptions change, then your mind has experienced spaciousness prior to the change, and that is what matters.

Perceiving things differently enhances your ability to be a fun and creative person. As you get better at opening, your spaciousness will increase, and you will find yourself spontaneously coming up with creative and humorous ideas.

INSTRUCTIONS FOR THE EXTENDED OPENING TECHNIQUE 1: "OUTER SPACE"

- Sit in a comfortable place. You will want to stay warm during the practice. Also make sure you are not likely to be disturbed, as distractions can be jarring.
- Remember your intention by thinking of your long-range goals for meditation, as well as your immediate goal for the session. Your immediate goal for an opening session is to allow your mind to experience a change in your perceptions.
- Practice a centering or attending technique until you feel relaxed. This will usually take only a couple of minutes.
- Then remember a time when you were in a place where you felt a sense of vastness. Places that people have described are: the ocean, the seashore, mountaintops, deserts, under the night sky, scuba diving. Focus your attention on the sense of vastness, of space all around you. As you experience that

sense of space around you, pretend that sounds, sights, and other sensations are moving farther and farther away. You can observe them, but they are at a distance.

- If your mind gets distracted by other phenomena, identify them and let them go. Return your awareness to the sense of vastness; it can help to imagine the distractions as moving farther and farther away. As you do that, you will find that you begin to feel changes in your perception of your body and other elements of what you are imagining.
- You may feel yourself moving upward, or shrinking, or expanding. Continue to keep your mind on the experience of vastness and accept these changes in your perception. As you continue to do this, you may find that the original image fades and you start having other images come, or even move into a dream state. Just continue to identify these and disengage from them. If your mind gets caught by them, then go back to the original image and your experience of vastness.
- At the end of the session, reflect on your experience and then gradually reorient yourself to your body, time, and place before you open your eyes.

INSTRUCTIONS FOR THE EXTENDED OPENING TECHNIQUE 2: "INNER SPACE"

- Sit in a comfortable place. You will want to stay warm during the practice. Also make sure you are not likely to be disturbed, as distractions can be jarring.
- Remember your intention by thinking of your long-range goals for meditation, as well as your immediate goal for the session. Your immediate goal for an opening session is to allow your mind to experience a change in your perceptions.
- Practice a centering or attending technique until you feel relaxed. This will usually take only a couple of minutes.

- Then observe the expansion and contraction of your chest and abdomen as you breathe in and out. Notice how they naturally expand as you inhale and contract as you exhale. Attend less to the movement of air and more to the expansion and contraction.
- Notice that it is hard to tell exactly where your body stops expanding and contracting. Some parts of your body are clearly moving and some are clearly still. However, the line between them is ambiguous. Experience that ambiguity, that confusion.
- Now imagine that the expansion and contraction are moving outward from your chest and abdomen into your shoulders, hips, arms, legs, and head. Imagine that your whole body is expanding and contracting gently as you breathe.
- If you get distracted, just identify the distraction, disengage from it, and go back to observing the sense of expansion and contraction. If you lose track of the experience of your whole body expanding and contracting, then go back to being aware of your chest and abdomen expanding and contracting.
- As you do this, you may have a sense that your body is changing position, shape, or size. When this happens, it is the result of experiencing spaciousness. Avoid analyzing the body perceptions and simply observe them.
- If thoughts or images go by, just observe them without trying to analyze them. Make note of them, and if you get caught up in them, just go back to being aware of expansion and contraction.
- At the end of the session, reflect on your experience. The experience of spaciousness comes from letting go of your usual way of sensing your body and allowing your mind to experience it differently. Make note of any images or thoughts that seemed particularly important. Then gradually

reorient to your whole body, time, and place before you open your eyes.

BRIEF OPENING PRACTICE: "INSTANT SPACE"

Like the other practices, opening has a brief version as well. The extended technique allows you to experience spaciousness in a way that radically changes your state of consciousness. Until you are used to that, such a change may be disorienting, making it difficult to do while involved in your other daily activities. In order to access spaciousness during the day, you need a brief opening technique that doesn't disorient you.

Being able to access spaciousness during the day is critically important for people who feel pressure from too many things to do. That includes most of us, most of the time. The pace of life seems to go faster and faster. We often feel crowded upon by the many things that are demanding our attention. Accessing spaciousness frequently during the day will give us relief from that feeling of pressure. While the demands will still be there, we will not feel them crowding in on us. Then we can deal with them more efficiently.

To do the brief opening technique, begin by remembering an experience of having a lot of space around you, or imagining such an experience. If you have experienced space or vastness in the extended sessions, you can remember that. Then take a deep breath in, pretending that there is a vast space inside your whole body and that the air is filling it. Then release the breath, imagining all that vast space flowing out and surrounding you, and that it is pushing all the things demanding your attention into the distance. That one breath can be enough, but you may want to repeat it one or two more times. We recommend that you limit this technique to three breaths so that you don't hyperventilate.

BRIAN'S EXPERIENCE WITH THE BRIEF OPENING PRACTICE

Brian is sitting at his desk, working on a presentation he has to make in a couple of hours. He is feeling some pressure about this, but feels sure that he will be ready in time. Then the phone rings. The caller informs him of a problem that needs his attention. As he hangs up the phone, a coworker comes into his cubicle and hands him a memo marked urgent. As he takes the memo, his computer signals him that he has another e-mail message. Brian feels his tension level leaping upward. His shoulders and jaw tense. His stomach tightens. His thoughts are angry and unprintable. It seems like everything is demanding his attention at once. He feels frustrated and angry.

Brian remembers the brief spaciousness exercise he has worked on for a few days. Space is exactly what he needs right now. He remembers his intention to experience a sense of space and then takes a deep breath in. As he does this, he imagines that his whole body is expanding, that the air is filling him like a balloon. He then releases the breath and imagines that everything around him is moving farther away.

Suddenly everything seems to calm down. Time seems to be moving slower. Brian realizes that he is still holding the memo he had been handed. Brian takes another deep breath in, imagining his body being filled with space. Then he exhales and imagines again that everything around him is moving farther away. Now he feels he has some breathing room and can think about the big picture. He has the presentation, the phone call, the e-mail, and the memo to deal with. As his mind scans these three tasks, he is able to prioritize intelligently. He really needs to do only a little more work on his presentation. He glances at the e-mail and realizes that he doesn't need to reply. There are a couple of people he can call to deal with the matter raised in the memo, and he can take care of the problem he had been informed of in the phone call. Brian feels reasonably comfortable. He has a lot to do in a short time, but he does not feel overwhelmed.

MARIA'S EXPERIENCE WITH THE BRIEF OPENING PRACTICE

Maria has picked up her children from day care after a stressful day at work. Her children are irritable and quarreling with each other. When she gets home, she finds a bunch of bills in the mailbox. As she urges her complaining children into the house, the phone rings. She rushes to get the phone, dropping the mail all over the floor. Her husband is calling to let her know that he will be delayed at work and won't be able to run the errands she asked him to. Just then her older child pushes the younger one onto the floor, who then proceeds to wail, "Mommy! She pushed me!"

Maria feels ready to explode. As she takes a deep breath to yell at her children, she suddenly remembers the spaciousness technique. She imagines feeling the breath filling her body. Her body seems to grow much bigger in response. That feels good. She releases the breath without yelling, but imagines that she is blowing the things around her away from her. That feels better. Maria repeats this during her next breath and now feels like she is standing taller and straighter.

Suddenly Maria experiences a shift. She doesn't have to take care of everything in the next two seconds. She hears her husband's voice over the phone, "Honey, are you OK?" She laughs and responds "Well, it's a little crazy here right now, but we're all right. I've got to run and deal with the kids. Love you, bye." She then picks up her younger child and instructs the older one to pick up the mail.

INSTRUCTIONS FOR THE BRIEF OPENING PRACTICE

- Remember your intention to experience a sense of increased space within and around you.
- Inhale and imagine that you are breathing in space as you inhale, that your whole body is expanding, and that the air is filling your whole body all the way out to your fingers and toes. (You do not have to close your eyes.)
- As you exhale, imagine that you are breathing out space and that everything around you is moving farther away. You are surrounded by space.
- The inhalation and exhalation should be easy and free. There is no need to strain to breathe deeply.
- The image of space within and without should come easily. Avoid straining to make it work.
- Repeat this for one or at most two more breaths and then reflect on your experience.

BRIAN'S RESULTS FROM OPENING PRACTICE

Brian has practiced the extended opening technique eight times over the past month. He interspersed his sessions of practicing opening with ones in which he practiced attending and concentrating. His experiences with opening have been varied. At first he found himself trying to re-create his first experience. This was frustrating, as the more he tried to create the sensations of floating upward, the more stuck he felt. The advice from his teacher was, **"The perceptual changes during opening occur when our mind lets go of its usual way of organizing the world. When that happens, our perceptions change. That change can be rather random, so it may not be the same change every time. If the desire to experience a particular change arises, identify it, disengage from it, and go back to experiencing the sense of vastness."**

Brian found that advice helpful. He could relate it to his difficulty with attending. He could see how practicing attending and getting better at letting go of distractions would also help him with opening. Once Brian accepted the fact that his experience will be varied, he found the opening practice to be very enjoyable. It became like taking a little vacation without having to pack any bags.

Brian finds the brief opening practice quite helpful. He is able to snap out of his automatic response to stressful situations when he is able to gain a sense of space around him. This is especially helpful when he is trying to keep his temper at home. When things upset him, he usually feels as if his focus is narrowing, like he is having tunnel vision. The brief practice seems to change this. His visual field opens up and his shoulders and chest relax. This changes his emotional response to one that is calmer and more reasonable. **"Opening creates room for responses that are different from your usual ones. This is why the brief practice is so important. When your temper is starting to get the best of you, opening enables you to see the situation differently. Then there is no need to lose your temper."**

MARIA'S RESULTS FROM OPENING PRACTICE

Maria has practiced the extended opening technique four times over the past month. She practiced concentrating and attending during the other eight extended practice sessions. Her initial experience with opening was so interesting and pleasant that she wanted to just practice opening. **"Opening can lead to very interesting and enjoyable experiences; however, you need to develop the other mental qualities to balance your mind. That means you must spend some sessions practicing attending and some sessions practicing concentrating, and not just practice opening."**

By interspersing the other practices with the opening sessions, Maria finds the other practices more enjoyable. She still finds the concentration sessions to be rather difficult, but the opening sessions seem to give her a rest and she is able to continue to make progress concentrating. Several times during opening practice, she experienced images that were unclear, and try as she might, she was unable to make them out. **"Remember, the opening practice is to help you experience spaciousness. You experience the spaciousness when your mind lets go of how it is organizing your perceptions. That occurs *before* the new images become clear. When the new images become clear, your mind is not using the spaciousness. It is using the other mental qualities to reorganize its perceptions. As you practice concentration and increase your clarity and steadiness, the new images will become clearer."** Maria feels that the opening sessions are the most enjoyable of all the practice sessions. They give her a sense of rest and ease that sometimes lasts for hours after the practice.

Maria finds the brief practice useful. She has been doing it a few times per day and experiences a sense of peace when she does it. She has also used it during meetings and finds that she does not get nearly as flustered. Often, when preparing to speak in a meeting, she has a sense of shrinking, as if the stares of the other people are compressing her. When she does the brief practice just before speaking, her perception changes and she feels a sense of expansion, as if she is large and the attention of the others is at a comfortable distance.

Maria has also played around with the opening technique for relaxation. She starts with the experience of expansion and contraction in her chest and abdomen. Then instead of allowing that sense to expand and spread over her whole body, she focuses the experience of expansion and contraction into specific areas of her body that feel tense. This causes a sense of letting go and space in that area. Maria has found that if she does a brief mental scan of her body before she eats lunch and uses the opening technique to relax areas that are tense, she feels much more relaxed while eating. Her stomach feels much more comfortable and she does not have difficulties with indigestion.

Both Brian and Maria are having success with the opening practices. However, they each feel that something is missing. The experiences during opening are enjoyable and restful, but seem to lack direction. They were worried about this and asked their teacher. The response was, **"It is natural for you to feel this way. Your mind has learned some skills and now it wants to use them. It is like a child who has learned to ride a bicycle and now wants to go places. You can now start to apply the mental abilities you have developed to specific goals you would like to achieve."**

REVIEW OF OPENING

Opening consists of becoming aware of a sense of vastness or space in a way that allows you to let go of the way you usually perceive the world. When you let go of your usual way of perceiving the world, you are using the mental quality of spaciousness. This spaciousness is often experienced as a sense of vastness within yourself.

After you let go, your mind will often reorganize your perceptions into a different experience. This can be experienced as imagery or as changes in your position or body size. Just accept these experiences as they arise, and keep letting go of them. You will learn how to use these experiences to help you move toward your goals later on. Right now just let them come and go.

You are not to practice opening every day. Balance the practice of opening with sessions where you practice attending or concentrating. As you practice concentration and attending, you will increase your ability to work with and use the images and other experiences that arise during opening.

Opening practice usually takes longer than fifteen minutes to complete comfortably, so we recommend a minimum of twenty minutes. That gives you time to get into the experience of spaciousness, enjoy it, and return to your usual way of experiencing the world.

You are having success with opening when you experience some change in your perception. This may occur with visual or auditory imagery. Or, you may have changes in your kinesthetic sense, a feeling that you are moving or changing size.

You must not try to achieve the same changes from session to session. Trying to experience a specific change in perception will impede the experience of opening. Just focus on the experience of vastness, or expansion and contraction, and then accept what happens.

The brief opening practice is helpful for bringing the effects of spaciousness into your daily life. It can be most useful for helping you deal with situations in which you feel very nervous or upset. It allows you to step back from the situation and gain a broader perspective.

TIPS FOR THE PRACTICE OF OPENING

- Remember your intention at the beginning of each session. This is especially important for opening practice, as your mind tends to drift when you are experiencing spaciousness. Remembering your intention will help it to drift in constructive directions.

- If you are having difficulty with distractions, identify them and disengage from them. Keep coming back to either the sensation of expansion and contraction or the sense of vastness.
- You can work with either or both of the techniques described. Play with them and use whichever one works best for you. You may find that one works well one day and the other works well another day.

6 recap: what you have learned so far

IN THE LAST four chapters, we introduced you to techniques from the four meditative practices of centering, attending, concentrating, and opening. The techniques you learned developed your mental qualities of steadiness, flexibility, warmth, clarity, and spaciousness. It usually takes students between three and six months to reach this point. Before we teach the applications in part 2, we would like to summarize the practices, the techniques, and the results you may be experiencing.

Please remember the brief techniques for each practice in addition to the extended techniques. You should spend at least ninety minutes per week with the extended techniques. If you practice the brief techniques as well, then you will make rapid progress even with that small an investment of time.

A summary of the brief and extended techniques presented for each meditative practice follows.

CENTERING

Definition. Maintaining continuous awareness of a physical or mental object. The object you maintain awareness of is called your center.

Purpose. Develops mental steadiness and prepares you to do the more complex techniques of attending and concentrating.

Extended Technique. Focus on the sensations in your lower abdomen. If you get distracted, return your awareness to those sensations.

Brief Technique. Focus on a simple mental phrase such as "Calm – Relaxed" or "Calm – Alert" for thirty to sixty seconds.

Success. You are ready to move on when you can maintain awareness of the sensations in your lower abdomen for thirty seconds without being distracted. For most people, this is the length of about five breaths.

Simple Application. Center on the mental phrase "Calm – Relaxed" for several minutes as you fall asleep.

Continued Practice. You do not need to practice the extended centering technique once you move on to the attending technique. However, you may continue to practice the brief technique several times per day for stress reduction.

ATTENDING

Definition. Identifying and disengaging from sensations, thoughts, and emotions.

Purpose. Develops mental flexibility and warmth.

Extended Technique. Focus on the sensations of air flowing in and out at the entrance of your nostrils or across your lips as you breathe. Identify and disengage from any distractions, returning your awareness to the sensations of air flowing in and out as you breathe.

Brief Technique. Observe what sensations, thoughts, and feelings are going through your mind. Spend only ten to twenty seconds recalling your experience for the preceding couple of minutes.

Success. Upon being distracted, you are able to return your awareness quickly and easily to the sensations of air flowing, and you can do this for fifteen minutes without feeling strained.

Simple Application. Center on different parts of your body in a progressive sequence. Identify and disengage from the sensations in each part before you move on to the next one. This can be extremely relaxing.

Continued Practice. After moving on to concentrating, you should continue with the extended attending technique for one-third of your extended practice sessions. You should practice the brief technique several times per day, three days per week.

CONCENTRATING

Definition. Maintaining intense awareness of an object and perceiving it in complete detail without being distracted.

Purpose. Develops mental steadiness and clarity.

Extended Technique. Start by concentrating on a simple physical shape, a simple sound, or a simple movement, and then shift to concentrating on the memory of that shape, sound, or movement.

Brief Technique. Concentrate for one to two minutes on the memory of an event that occurred earlier in the day.

Success. You are able to hold the mental image steady and perceive its details for ten seconds.

Continued Practice. After moving on to the opening technique, continue to practice the extended concentrating technique for one-third of your extended practice sessions. You should also practice the brief technique two or three times per day, four days per week.

OPENING

Definition. Letting go of how the mind organizes perceptions so that a different perspective can arise.

Purpose. Develops mental spaciousness.

Extended Technique 1. Feel your chest and abdomen expand as you inhale and contract as you exhale. Imagine that your whole body is expanding and contracting as you breathe in and out.

Extended Technique 2. Imagine being in a wide-open place such as on a mountaintop. Imagine that everything is very far away, and feel your mind filling the vastness.

Brief Technique. Take a deep breath in and imagine it filling your whole body with lots of space. As you breathe out, imagine that the space is surrounding you and that everything is moving farther away.

Success. You experience a change in body awareness, position sense, or a change in how time passes.

Continued Practice. Until you start practicing the applications, do the extended opening technique in one-third of your extended sessions. Practice the brief technique several times every day.

BRIAN'S RESULTS FROM PRACTICING THE FOUR BASIC TECHNIQUES

It has been almost five months since Brian had the talk with his sister, Karen, in which she advised him to meditate. He took her advice, and has been practicing consistently for the past four and a half months. During a family get-together, the two of them have some time together.

Karen says, "We haven't talked in a while. How are you doing? You seem better than you did a few months ago."

Brian replies, "I am better. I'm a lot more hopeful."

"That's good. Do you mind telling me what's changed?"

Brian smiles self-consciously, "Well, I took your advice."

"Really!" jokes his sister.

"Yes, I actually started meditating about five months ago. It has been a big help."

"I'm glad to hear that. What have you noticed that has changed?" Karen asked.

"Hmm. For one thing, I feel more relaxed about things. The pressure at work hasn't changed, but I don't feel as exhausted by it. I also seem to feel more rested on my days off."

"So, the meditation is helping you relax?" she queried.

Brian replied, "It's more than that. I feel less irritable, I'm not as stressed out. I feel like I can see things from someone else's point of view, not just my own."

"That sounds good, anything else?"

Brian reflected, "I seem to be more accepting of change. If something goes wrong and I have to change plans, I don't feel as upset about it and can change my plans constructively. Here's an example: One day John [Brian's fourteen-year-old son] and I were supposed to go to a ball game. Unfortunately, the car broke down two blocks away. Ordinarily I would have been completely upset and lost my temper. Instead I took a deep breath. While I was disappointed, I stayed calm. After getting the car towed to the shop, John and I decided to go to the park and throw a ball around. Then we went and had ice cream together. It turned out to be a great day for the two of us."

"Brian, that's fantastic!"

"You know, it's not so much that things have changed. I've changed. My mind is working better for me. I remember things better and I have more creative ideas. I have more influence over my moods and reactions. I have a lot more hope and peace than I used to. I don't feel stuck anymore."

"So are you going to continue practicing?"

"Yes. I'm comfortable with the basic techniques now and will be starting the application of them. After seeing so much benefit from just the basics, I'm looking forward to experiencing what I can achieve with the applications."

MARIA'S RESULTS FROM PRACTICING THE FOUR BASIC TECHNIQUES

It has been four months since Maria and Susan had their conversation about the possibility of Maria trying meditation. Since that time they have chatted only briefly, but they arranged to meet again for lunch today so they could talk.

After the two had chatted over lunch awhile, Susan commented, "You seem to be more relaxed these days. Are you feeling better?"

Maria smiled. "I am, thank you. I have to admit that your suggestion that I practice meditation was a lifesaver."

"Well, I'm glad to hear that. You must have gotten over your fears about meditation being too Eastern."

"Yes, it doesn't feel strange at all," Maria replied. "The techniques make sense, and I'm certainly not practicing a different religion."

"What about the time commitment?" Susan asked.

"That took some getting used to at first, but I was able to find ways to fit it into my day. Kevin was at first a little reluctant to work with me on this, but he is seeing so much positive change in me that now he is happy to give me the time."

"Are you using the brief techniques?" Susan inquired.

Maria replied, "The brief techniques are so helpful. I am surprised at how much benefit I get from doing those short exercises. Without them, I don't think I would have made the progress I did."

"What did you find most helpful?" Susan asked.

Maria laughed. "You know, I used to think that I was crazy because of the way I would get scattered, frustrated, and irritable when I was stressed. Just hearing that it might be an imbalance in how I use the qualities of my mind, and that this could be corrected by simple exercises, was such a relief."

"How empowering!"

"And now I am so different," Maria continued. "I can't believe how much more coherent I feel. I used to get scattered so easily. Now I can stay focused, prioritize, and deal with things. I still get emotional, but I can keep my feelings from exploding out of me."

"It sounds like you have made some big changes," said Susan.

"I'm definitely more peaceful. You know, one day my deadline on a project had been moved up. So instead of being ahead, I was behind. I had to stay late at work, and you can imagine how stressed I felt. When I got home, Kevin was irritable, the sink had backed up, and the kids were fighting. I was starting to get the old feeling of running on a treadmill. Ordinarily I would have tried to fix everything at once, gotten completely overwhelmed, then become irritable and developed a headache. Instead I took a deep breath and told everyone I needed absolute silence for five minutes. That surprised them so much that I actually got it. During that five minutes, I was able to become calm and alert. I was able to disengage from the thoughts about work because I couldn't do anything about it anyway at the time. At the end of the five minutes, my mind was clear. I told Kevin that he would be responsible for dealing with the sink. I would take the kids and we would stay out of his hair for the next couple of hours. I thought the kids would be a challenge, but we went into the living room and tickled each other for the next half hour. Then I read stories for a while. After that the kids had calmed down enough to go play by themselves. Kevin was able to fix the sink during that time and he was feeling good. We actually got to sit together quietly for a little while before we had to start the dinner routine. It was such a different outcome from what usually would have happened."

"Much more enjoyable, I imagine," Susan said.

"That's right. And these changes are just happening. I simply focus on my goals and do the exercises, and my life is straightening out. Instead of life being stressful, it's just challenging. I'm becoming a better person. That is what makes me excited about starting the applications."

PART II
applying meditation in your daily life

BY NOW YOU will have gained enough familiarity with the basic practices to start applying them. You know that centering involves placing your awareness on something. You have experienced how to identify thinking, sensing, and feeling, and to disengage from thoughts, sensations, and emotions while attending. You know the intense focus on details that concentrating gives you. You have felt the changes in perception that accompany opening.

You have already discovered the benefits that come from simply strengthening and balancing your five mental qualities. You are prepared to begin to use those enhanced mental abilities to move more directly toward your goals.

The principles that you used to succeed with the basic techniques are also required for succeeding with the applications. You will learn both extended techniques and brief techniques. You will need to perform each of the three phases—intention, execution, and reflection—during each of the application techniques.

In addition to practicing the application techniques, you should also spend a little time working on the basics. The applications also develop the five mental qualities, but keeping up with the basics will be better than just practicing the applications alone. It is like being a gymnast, who spends time stretching before practicing any routine. Such stretching exercises are basic, and they improve the gymnast's flexibility much more than simply practicing routines for competition would.

We recommend that you spend one-third of your extended sessions practicing one of the basic techniques. If you are doing three extended sessions per week, then you would spend one of those sessions doing a basic technique. You may rotate through the extended attending, concentrating, and opening techniques in turn. So, if you were doing one basic extended session per week, then you would do the basic attending technique the first week, the basic concentrating technique the second week, and the basic opening technique the third week. Another method to balance your practice is to keep a journal in which you record the technique you practice during each session. Then you can review your record periodically and adjust what you practice so that you train your mind in a balanced manner.

In this section, we describe applications of meditation that will enhance key parts of your life, beginning with your physical health and progressing on to your performance, your relationships, and your spirituality. However, unlike part 1, you do not need to complete working with the techniques from one chapter before you go on to the next. Each chapter describing the applications contains three techniques. Within each chapter you should practice the techniques in order, as each builds on the previous one.

7 health: strengthening your mind-body-spirit connection

THE MIND AND the body are intimately connected and affect each other. We can influence the way the mind affects the body by shifting our awareness. To experience this, perform the following experiment. Notice how moist or dry your mouth is right now. Now imagine a big juicy lemon sitting on a table in front of you. Imagine that there is a knife next to the lemon. Now imagine cutting the lemon in half. Then imagine that you lift one of the lemon halves as you open your mouth and you take a big bite of the lemon, sinking your teeth deeply into its pulp. If anything happens in your mouth as you imagine this, then you are experiencing changing your body by shifting your awareness.

Since your mind, body, and spirit are connected, meditation can help you strengthen that connection and influence it in a positive way. As your mind-body-spirit connection becomes stronger and more positive, you experience a sense of physical peace. You move more efficiently, your breathing and heartbeat are calmer, and you feel more harmony inside yourself. By applying the meditative practices of centering, attending, concentrating, and opening, your mind will have a powerful, positive effect on your body.

You don't need to wait for something to go wrong before you work on improving your health. After all, you don't wait for your car's engine to burn up before you change its oil. Why should you wait for your body to burn out before you start to take care of it? The exercises you will learn are excellent for improving your state of health.

Before we introduce you to the three health applications in this chapter, we want to make a couple of points. The first one is that meditation is not to be used as a cure-all. It is not meant to replace medical treatment. In fact, trying to treat a serious medical condition with meditation alone is dangerous. If you are receiving treatment from a physician, you can continue to receive that treatment and use the exercises we describe. If you are having symptoms, then we urge you to speak with a physician about them and not treat them only with meditation. Meditation can certainly augment standard medical treatments, but it should *never* be used as a substitute for them.

People with mental disorders can be especially prone to thinking that meditation alone will cure them. However, since meditation exercises the mind, people with mental disorders can feel strained from the effects of meditation. Those people need to realize that professional mental health treatment and even medications will be helpful. Medication and therapy can augment the benefits of meditation.

The second point we need to make is that if you get sick, it is not necessarily your fault. We believe that a lot of damage is done when people are told that they have caused their own illness. There is a lot of randomness to illness. Some people who smoke live to an old age, and others get lung cancer and die at fifty. Our minds are good at finding "reasons" for things. But none of the emotional "reasons" for why certain people get a particular illness has held up under scientific research. There are mean, hurtful people who will live to be ninety. There are wonderfully spiritual people who will die young.

Meditation is to be used to help you find peace. If you are sick, you are not to blame yourself for causing your illness. Most illnesses have varied causes, many of which are outside of our control. Even if you become spiritually "perfect," your body is simply not going to last forever. Meditation can help your body stay healthier for a longer period of time. And when it is time for you to leave your body, meditation can help even that transition to be peaceful.

We will introduce you to three health applications in this chapter. The first one, Autonomic Relaxation, uses centering and attending skills to evoke a deep state of relaxation. The second, Inner Harmony, uses attending and concentrating skills to create a more positive relationship between you and your body. The third, Inner Light, uses attending, concentrating, and opening skills to bring healing energy into your body.

HEALTH APPLICATION 1: AUTONOMIC RELAXATION

Physicians divide the nervous system into two general parts. The voluntary nervous system is the one that is under your conscious control. Right now you are using it to turn the pages of this book. The voluntary nervous system is the part of your nervous system you use to interact in a deliberate way with your environment.

The other part of your nervous system is the autonomic, or involuntary, nervous system. It is the nervous system that you do not influence consciously, unless you have practiced techniques like those you are about to learn. The autonomic nervous system controls your resting muscle tension, your skin temperature, your heart rate, your breathing (most of the time), and the activity of your digestive tract. It also affects your immune system, your hormone production, and many other physical processes. When people think of relaxation, they think of reducing their muscle tension. However, muscular relaxation is only one part of the autonomic nervous system. Autonomic Relaxation relaxes five parts of the autonomic nervous system, giving you a deeper and more thorough experience of relaxation. The instructions we give are similar to those given in numerous books under the term "autogenic exercises"; however, the instructions we give contain some important differences.

BRIAN'S FIRST EXPERIENCE WITH AUTONOMIC RELAXATION

Brian has already gained some health benefits from the basic techniques, but he wants more results and is going to practice some meditation techniques for improving his health. He will be starting with Autonomic Relaxation. He wanted to start with a more complex exercise, but his teacher said, **"The first health application is Autonomic Relaxation. That will produce a deeply relaxed state that increases the body's self-healing abilities. Autonomic Relaxation is also a stepping-stone to more complex techniques."**

As Brian sits down for his morning session, he feels a little cool. He gets a blanket and drapes it around himself to feel more comfortable. He then remembers his intention by remembering his goals for meditation and especially his goals for improving his health: reducing his neck tension and lowering his blood pressure.

Brian then begins the execution phase. He relaxes briefly by thinking "Calm" as he breathes in and "Relaxed" as he breathes out. After a couple of breaths he feels his muscles loosen. Now that he has started to relax, he centers on the phrase "My arms and legs are heavy and warm." As he does this, he attends to the sensations in his arms and legs. He feels his arms from the shoulders all the way to the fingertips. He feels his legs from the hips all the way to the toes. As he attends to the sensations in his arms and legs, he continues to center on the thought "My arms and legs are heavy and warm," repeating that phrase over and over in his mind at a comfortable pace.

Brian notices that his hands feel rather cold, and some discouraging thoughts come up. "I'm not doing it right. This is not working." He remembers, **"Let your body do whatever your body wants to do. If your arms do not feel heavy or warm, that is OK. The key to this exercise is to 'think and let.' You think the thought, and let your body do what it wants. If other thoughts come up, just identify them as thoughts and disengage from them. Return to centering on the thought 'My arms and legs are heavy and warm,' and accept whatever sensations you are aware of."** Fortunately, Brian has had enough practice with attending to disengage from the discouraging thoughts. He continues to center on the thought "My arms and legs are heavy and warm." After about another minute he suddenly notices that his right hand feels somewhat warm and comfortable.

Brian continues to think "My arms and legs are heavy and warm" for a couple of minutes, while simply paying attention to the sensations in his arms and legs. Both arms and both legs feel a little heavy and his right arm has become comfortably warm. He can also feel a soft, comfortable pulsing in his fingers. It is time to move on to the next step, but he is tempted to continue this one in order to experience more heaviness and warmth in his arms and legs. **"You need to move to the next step after a couple of minutes, even if you do not notice any results. If you extend one step to get more results, you train your body to respond slowly. You also risk trying to get results and losing the 'think and let' attitude. So move on—the results will come when your body is ready."**

Brian stops centering on the thought "My arms and legs are heavy and warm" and takes a couple of comfortable breaths. He then begins to think, "My chest is calm and peaceful. My chest is calm and peaceful. My chest is calm and peaceful." As he centers on this thought, he pays attention to the sensations in his chest. He is quite calm, and immediately feels a pleasant pulsing in his chest area.

Suddenly he realizes that he is feeling tense and is having worried thoughts about the state of his heart and his high blood pressure. **"When you center on the phrase for the chest, you may have anxieties about the state of your heart. Simply identify those thoughts and disengage from them as you go back to centering on the phrase 'My chest is calm and peaceful.'"**

Brian identifies the anxious thoughts and goes back to centering on the phrase "My chest is calm and peaceful." He feels the tension decrease and remembers the advice **"Think and let things happen. Your body will take care of you. Center on the phrases gently, attend to the sensations, and trust your body's wisdom."** After a couple of minutes, Brian lets go of the thought "My chest is calm and peaceful," and moves on to the next step.

He takes a couple of deep breaths and centers on the thought "My breath is free and easy. My breath is free and easy. My breath is free and easy." As he does so, he pays attention to the sensations in the lower part of his chest, the circular area around the lower edge of his rib cage.

Brian notices that he feels very comfortable and that his breathing is very peaceful. He is enjoying this exercise immensely. After a couple of minutes, he lets go of the thought "My breath is free and easy," and begins to center on the phrase "My abdomen is warm and comfortable. My abdomen is warm and comfortable. My abdomen is warm and comfortable." As he does this, he attends to the sensations in his abdomen. This is easy for him, and after a couple of minutes Brian feels the warmth from his abdomen spread all over his body.

Brian moves on to the final step by centering on the thought "My face is soft and gentle." He feels calm and peaceful all over. His eyes relax and the muscles of his forehead and cheeks smooth out. The corners of his mouth turn up slightly and his jaw loosens. Brian realizes that he usually presents a hard exterior to the world and this hardness has become a habit, continuing even when he doesn't need it. It feels good to soften his appearance. He enjoys the feeling of a soft smile upon his face, and that deepens the feeling of peace all over his body.

Brian continues to center on the phrase "My face is soft and gentle," enjoying the sensations in his face. After a couple of minutes he lets go of that thought and just enjoys the feeling of deep relaxation throughout his body.

Brian moves into the reflection phase of the exercise by reviewing his experience. He remembers that he has to avoid trying to achieve results and just accept his body's response as he centers on the different phrases in turn. He notices how warm and comfortable he feels all over and then gradually reorients himself to time and place. He then takes a deep breath and opens his eyes. **"After doing a deep relaxation exercise, remember to get up slowly so that your body has time to adjust to the change in activity."** Brian remembers this advice and wiggles his fingers and toes before he sits upright, then stretches his arms and legs before he gets up from the pillow.

MARIA'S FIRST EXPERIENCE WITH AUTONOMIC RELAXATION

Maria has been looking forward to doing the health applications. While the basic exercises have helped some, she wants to get more benefit. As she begins her afternoon session, she starts by focusing on her intention: fewer headaches. She then centers on the phrase "My arms and legs are heavy and warm" while attending to the sensations in her arms. After a few seconds, her mind starts jumping around. She disengages from the distracting thoughts, but they return almost immediately. Maria feels frustrated, but then remembers, **"It is OK to have other thoughts during the exercise. Just let the phrase you are centering on be present, as if it were a radio in the background."** Maria finds this helpful and feels her frustration ease.

After a couple of minutes centering on "My arms and legs are warm and heavy," Maria feels more relaxed. She moves on to the next phrase, "My chest is calm and peaceful," while attending to the sensations in her chest. Again she has to disengage from distracting thoughts, but is able to stay centered.

As Maria centers on the next phrase, "My breath is free and easy," she notices that her breaths are varying in speed and depth. She wonders if she is doing the exercise correctly because she thought she should breathe deeply if she were relaxed. **"Just let your body breathe the way it wants to. Sometimes as you relax, your body finds that shorter and shallower breaths are more efficient than slow deep breaths. So the rate and depth of breathing is not directly related to how relaxed you are. Just let the body breathe however it wants."** When she remembers that, Maria is able to disengage from the worries about her breath and enjoy the feeling of ease and peace this gives her. After centering on the thought "My breath is free and easy" for a couple of minutes, she also realizes that her arms are quite comfortable. They have continued to become warmer while she was centering on the other phrases.

When Maria centers on the phrase "My abdomen is warm and comfortable," she notices that her abdomen actually feels a little bloated and crampy. She tries to continue to center on the phrase, but it feels forced. **"If the body part associated with the phrase feels uncomfortable, avoid forcing yourself to attend to sensations from that area. Just center on the phrase for a couple of seconds and then move on."**

Maria lets go of trying to pay attention to her abdomen and moves to the last phrase of the exercise, "My face is soft and gentle." This feels very nice and seems to reinforce the effect of the previous phrases. Her body feels relaxed from her skin all the way down to her core.

Maria reflects on the experience and remembers how many distracting thoughts she had. She realizes they did not keep her from doing the exercise and were just a minor annoyance. Maria reorients herself to time and place and then wiggles her fingers and toes as she ends the exercise.

INSTRUCTIONS FOR HEALTH APPLICATION 1: AUTONOMIC RELAXATION

This exercise requires proficiency with centering and attending. You will be centering on a mental phrase while attending to sensations. You can start this exercise after you are familiar with the basic exercises from chapters 2 and 3.

- Start by remembering your intention. Recall the goals you have for meditation, especially those that are health-related.
- Start the execution phase of the exercise by using the brief centering technique from chapter 2, centering on the thought "Calm" as you inhale and "Relaxed" as you exhale. Do this for about five breaths so that your body settles down a little.
- Then notice your arms, from the shoulders to the fingertips. Also notice your legs, from the hips to the toes. Gently attend to the sensations in your arms and legs as you center on the thought "My arms and legs are heavy and warm." The focus of your awareness is the thought. You are only peripherally aware of the sensations in your arms and legs. Accept whatever sensations you experience in your arms and legs and continue to center on the thought "My arms and legs are

heavy and warm." If you get distracted by other thoughts or sensations, disengage from these and go back to your center. After about two to four minutes, let go of the thought and just enjoy a couple of nice easy breaths.

- Now move your awareness to the sensations in your chest. Then center on the thought "My chest is calm and peaceful." Again, the focus of your awareness is the thought, and you are to attend to the sensations in your chest in a peripheral manner. Identify them and let them happen. If other thoughts or sensations come in, simply notice them, disengage from them, and go back to centering on the thought "My chest is calm and peaceful." After about two to four minutes, let go of the thought and take a couple of nice easy breaths.

- Now move your awareness to the circular area at the lower edge of your rib cage. This is the place near where your diaphragm is attached. Notice how the sensations there change as you inhale and exhale. Then center on the thought "My breath is free and easy." Continue to be gently aware of the sensations at the lower edge of your ribs as you center on the thought "My breath is free and easy." After about two to four minutes let go of the thought and just enjoy a couple of nice easy breaths.

- Next move your awareness to your abdomen. Feel your abdomen from the lower part of the ribs down to the pelvic bones. Also notice how your abdomen is not just in front but extends to the sides and around the back as well. Attend to these sensations as you center on the thought "My abdomen is warm and comfortable." After two to four minutes allow yourself to enjoy whatever feelings of peace you are experiencing.

- Next move your awareness to your face as you center on the phrase "My face is soft and gentle." Center on this phrase for at least two minutes, continuing for as long as you like.

- When you are ready to stop, reflect on your experience. Remember what it was like to center on the different thoughts while watching the sensations and accepting whatever happened. This is called a "think and let" state. In this state you are doing something, without caring about the results.

TIPS FOR THE PRACTICE OF AUTONOMIC RELAXATION

- Avoid trying to get particular results. If you are feeling anxiety about getting results, focus more strongly on the mental phrase and pay less attention to the physical sensations.
- If a particular phrase causes difficulty, then move on to the next one.
- If you have any discomfort from a particular phrase, then do not use it.
- If you are being treated for a medical disorder, you must let your physician know that you are doing these exercises so that any effects can be monitored.

BRIAN'S RESULTS FROM AUTONOMIC RELAXATION PRACTICE

Brian has been practicing autonomic relaxation for four fifteen-minute sessions per week over the past month. During the sessions he has noticed that he is now relaxing more quickly, more deeply, and more consistently. He is also feeling a much greater sense of ease in his neck and shoulders. At his last doctor's visit his blood pressure was still above normal, but it had dropped slightly. His doctor agreed to just watch it for a while before starting any medication.

Brian has also learned to use a short version of Autonomic Relaxation at work. He leans back in his desk chair and spends about twenty to thirty seconds centering on each phrase. This short version takes only two minutes and he feels quite relaxed from it. He does this exercise three or four times per day. These breaks are increasing his mental efficiency and reducing his fatigue.

MARIA'S RESULTS FROM AUTONOMIC RELAXATION PRACTICE

Maria has practiced Autonomic Relaxation twice per week for the past two weeks. She does the exercise for about thirty minutes after work. She finds it does relax her, but her mind still gets quite distracted after centering on a phrase for more than about a minute. She described her difficulties to her teacher, who said, **"Your mind wants to be active, and that is why it is jumping around. However, you are experiencing enough relaxation to move on to the next exercise, and that will fit your active mind better than this one does."** Maria is able to experience a sense of inner relaxation, and the phrase "My face is soft and gentle" feels really good to her. She uses it as a brief centering exercise during the day and finds it lightens her moods.

HEALTH APPLICATION 2: INNER HARMONY

Inner Harmony builds on Autonomic Relaxation and creates a mental state in which we increase the harmony among our body's different systems.

Most of us have a poor relationship with our bodies. We think of our bodies in very critical terms. We find fault with our size, our shape, our looks, and on and on.

Spend a little time attending to the thoughts about your body that go through your mind. Are they warm, friendly, complimentary thoughts? Or are they harsh, critical, and even abusive ones? What if you lived with someone who was as critical of you as you are of your body? How would you react if you were complimented or thanked as rarely as you compliment or thank your body?

In the exercise of Inner Harmony, you will apply your concentrating and attending skills to developing a warm, accepting, and loving relationship with your body. When your body feels appreciated, then it works more harmoniously with you. All the systems in the body will work more harmoniously as well.

To do the Inner Harmony technique, you start with the experience of relaxation you obtained from the Autonomic Relaxation exercise. Then you concentrate on a sense of appreciation and gratitude. As you concentrate on that sense of appreciation and gratitude, you think about the processes your body carries out. You think about how all the various parts of your body participate in these processes to keep you alive and healthy.

The processes are respiration, digestion, purification, sensation, expression, and regulation. You do not need to know all the details about how those processes work. Your body knows the details better than anyone, and you can trust it. You simply need to think about each process in turn while concentrating on the feeling of appreciation and gratitude for each.

By concentrating on appreciation and gratitude while thinking about the various processes your body performs, you strengthen those systems and facilitate their working together.

BRIAN'S FIRST EXPERIENCE WITH INNER HARMONY

Brian is beginning an Inner Harmony session after a month of practicing Autonomic Relaxation, which he greatly enjoyed. He remembers his intention to feel more healthy and then begins the execution stage by taking two minutes to go rapidly through Autonomic Relaxation. As he centers on the phrase "My face is soft and gentle," he feels very quiet and peaceful inside. Brian then thinks about feeling love and gratitude for his body. Nothing much seems to come to him. He just feels quiet inside. There really isn't a lot of emotion. **"If your mind is so quiet that it doesn't feel appreciation and gratitude, then you have to wake it up a bit. Think about having a body and what would happen if you didn't have one. This can generate more energy."** Brian realizes that he is glad that his body works as well as it does. He doesn't usually think about it and tends to take it for granted. He scans his body mentally and feels warm and happy about it.

As Brian thinks about the process of respiration, he feels somewhat uncomfortable. His mind doesn't want to think about all the details. It just wants to stay with the warm and happy feeling. **"When doing this exercise you are bringing a feeling of appreciation to the processes your body performs. You don't need to think about the parts. The essence of the process of respiration is the generation of energy. Just think about your body generating energy."** Brian finds it easier to think about energy instead of lots of body parts he doesn't know about. He thinks about how all the cells in his body use energy and feels thankful that they are able to do that. After a couple of minutes he feels a little tingly all over.

Brian moves to the next process, digestion. He remembers to focus on the process and not the parts. He thinks about his cells getting nutrients and experiences a sense of fullness. He then focuses on the process of purification, thinking about how his body cleanses itself of things that are harmful. He feels love and gratitude toward his body for doing that. After a few minutes, he feels as if a cleansing fluid is washing through him.

When Brian moves to the next process, sensation, he begins to feel a little tired. He is finding the Inner Harmony exercise difficult and prefers the Autonomic Relaxation. He wants to stop thinking about all these processes and just rest in a state of quiet and relaxation. **"If your mind has a lot of natural steadiness, you will like Autonomic Relaxation more. However, this practice has some benefits that Autonomic Relaxation does not have. If you are feeling tired, just move through the systems more quickly."** Brian thinks briefly about the different sensory processes and how grateful he is that he can see, hear, touch, taste, and smell. After a couple of minutes, he focuses on the process of expression, and then moves to the process of regulation. He finds that the exercise feels more effective if he thinks about each process briefly and then recenters on the feeling of peace, gratitude, and love with a smile on his face.

MARIA'S FIRST EXPERIENCE WITH INNER HARMONY

Maria has been encouraged by the positive change in her health so far. She has practiced Autonomic Relaxation for a couple of weeks. She is able to move through the different phrases rapidly, and during the day has used "My face is soft and gentle" as a brief technique. She is looking forward to the next exercise, Inner Harmony.

Maria starts by remembering her intention. She recalls her goals for meditation and specifically her goals of improving her health and having fewer headaches.

Maria starts the execution phase by going rapidly through the Autonomic Relaxation exercise. She spends a few seconds centering on each of the first five phrases. She has been practicing this exercise for a couple of weeks, so she is able to relax quickly. She then centers on the phrase "My face is soft and gentle" for a couple of minutes to deepen the sense of peace and relaxation.

Maria now thinks about how much work her body does for her and how thankful she is for that. She feels appreciation and gratitude for her body, and as her smile deepens, she feels even more peaceful.

Maria then begins to think about different bodily processes in turn. She first reflects on the process of respiration, by which her body takes in oxygen and uses it to produce energy. She thinks about how her lungs and diaphragm work together to breathe in the oxygen. She thinks about how her blood cells pick up the oxygen and how her heart pumps the blood to all parts of the body.

Maria starts to feel she is losing the sense of peace and gratitude as she gets more involved in thinking about the process of respiration. **"Continue to reinforce the sense of appreciation and gratitude by returning your awareness to the feeling of gentleness in your face and eyes. Let those sensations anchor you to the more abstract idea of love and thankfulness for your body."**

Maria returns her awareness to her face, which is smiling softly, and the emotions of appreciation and gratitude. She then goes back to reflecting on the process of respiration, realizing that the oxygen that is delivered to the cells is used by them to produce energy— energy that helps them live and carry out their functions. She suddenly has the sense that all her cells are humming happily as they use the oxygen brought to them by the blood, and that her lungs, heart, and blood vessels are humming as well, in tune with her cells.

Maria then lets go of thinking about the process of respiration and returns to her feeling of gratitude by focusing her attention on the sensation of smiling in her face. After a couple of comfortable breaths, she moves on to the next process, digestion.

Maria thinks about the process by which her body extracts nutrients from food and sends them to all the cells in her body. As she starts thinking about all the organs involved in digestion, she starts to worry that she doesn't know enough about them. **"You do not need to know all the body parts involved. Think about the process, the idea of digestion, and not all the biochemical steps."**

Maria lets go of struggling to remember all the digestive organs and thinks about the activity they all contribute to: extracting the nutrients from the food she eats, converting them into forms her cells can use, and transporting them all over her body. She develops a feeling of satisfaction, as if her cells are comfortable and satiated.

Maria then lets go of thinking about digestion and moves on to the next process, purification. This is the process by which her body gets rid of everything that is useless or harmful, and by which it replaces worn-out parts. The first things that leap to mind is her intestines and kidneys, which excrete solid and liquid waste. This seems to be a distasteful idea; however, she quickly realizes that she is thankful for those organs, as she would be very uncomfortable if they did not do their work correctly. **"If you feel some aversion toward a particular process or body part, then you need to work on bringing appreciation and gratitude there. Reinforce your connection to the love and gratitude by being aware of the smile on your face."**

Maria reinforces her sense of gratitude by focusing her attention on the gentle smile on her face, and then continues to think about the process of purification. She realizes that her immune cells are part of this process because they get rid of harmful invaders. They also break down old, worn-out cells, making room for the body to replace them. As she experiences appreciation for the process of purification, Maria feels a sense of cleansing, as if some fluid or energy is washing through her. She considers that even her skin gets rid of salts, so it, too, is involved in this purification process. She enjoys the feeling of cleansing, and now feels even more peaceful.

Maria then thinks about the process of sensation. She thinks briefly about each of the different senses. She feels grateful for her ability to see, hear, smell, taste, and touch. She reflects on how each of these senses brings joy to her life. She appreciates her ability to sense the beauty around her. As she experiences this, she feels more connected to her world.

Maria thinks about the process of expression. She reflects on the different ways she expresses herself and how her body helps her do that. At first she is confused about the parts of the body that contribute to that process. **"You use your muscles, bones, and the connections between them to move, speak, draw, write, and perform all other activities by which you communicate."** As Maria reflects on this, she realizes that even her breathing muscles are involved in the process of expression because they bring in the air that she uses to speak with. She remembers hearing that her vocal cords are muscles as well and that their relaxation and contraction changes the pitch of her voice. She thinks about her smile, and realizes that it comes from the way her muscles on her face move. She feels a new appreciation for her body and her muscles. She had thought of muscles as important only for lifting weight, and more masculine. Now, however, she sees them as the means by which she expresses herself. The thought of muscles being feminine is new to her. Maria feels a sense of warmth flow through her and feels a friendliness with her body that she hasn't felt before.

Maria moves to the last process in the exercise, that of regulation. She reflects on all the different processes that are going on at once inside her and how she is also aware of and communicating with the world outside of her body. She thinks about how all these processes are regulated so that they work harmoniously. She realizes that communication among all the different cells in her body is a vital part of this process. **"It is very likely that every cell in our body receives some form of information from every other cell. The different body parts are not isolated. Our bodily processes communicate with one another constantly."** Maria reflects on how often she feels as if she is isolated from her body, or how she dislikes certain parts of her body. She realizes that all parts of her body are intimately connected with one another. She thinks about how they must communicate with one another to regulate their activity into a harmonious flow. As Maria does this, she feels warm and accepting of her whole physical being. She has the image of how interconnected all its elements are and how many different processes flow in cycles. She thinks about the different daily and monthly cycles she goes through and reflects on the extraordinary internal communication that regulates those. Maria feels as if her body is humming like a networked computer system, everything inside communicating with everything else.

Maria rests in this peaceful state for some time before her alarm beeps at her. She then reflects on the wonderful sense of gratitude she feels for her body. She thinks about how most of the time she takes her body for granted, noticing it only to scold it for something. In contrast, this experience feels quite pleasant, and she plans on practicing the Inner Harmony technique frequently.

INSTRUCTIONS FOR HEALTH APPLICATION 2: INNER HARMONY

- Start with the Autonomic Relaxation exercise. You should be able to move through all the phrases, getting some relaxation from each, within two to five minutes.
- While you center on "My face is soft and gentle," think about love and gratitude. You can connect more with this sense of love and gratitude by remembering a time when you felt these emotions.
- You will know you are successful when you feel a soft smile appear effortlessly on your face.

- Once you feel love and gratitude, think about how grateful you are for having a body. Thank your body for being there and staying alive for you.
- Concentrate on the emotions of love and gratitude while you think about each of the following processes in turn. If you get distracted from the sense of love and gratitude, refresh your memory by returning your awareness to the smile on your face.
- As you think about the processes detailed below, do not worry if you are unsure of all the different parts involved. Just as you can enjoy music without knowing exactly how all the instruments work, you can feel gratitude for your bodily processes without knowing all the anatomy and physiology involved.
- Concentrate on the following processes for two to four minutes in turn:

  — *Respiration.* This is the process by which your body produces energy. The lungs, heart, and blood are involved of course. All your body cells are also involved because they use oxygen, sugar, and fat to generate energy. Imagine that each cell in your body is a little power plant generating energy.

  — *Digestion.* This is the process by which your body extracts nutrients from your food and delivers them to the cells. The body parts involved are the mouth, teeth, stomach, and intestines. The liver and pancreas also help by making chemicals that assist in digesting the food. The heart and blood help by transporting the nutrients all over the body. Think about how all the cells in your body are receiving the nutrients they need.

  — *Purification.* This is the process by which your body gets rid of everything that is useless or harmful to it. It also includes the processes by which your body replaces worn-out parts. The most obvious organs involved are the kidneys and intestines. However, the lungs are involved because they breathe out carbon dioxide. The immune system has an important role in purification because it is constantly cleansing the body of harmful organisms. Think about the process of cleansing that is constantly going on throughout the body.

— *Sensation.* This includes the processes by which you receive information from the world around you. Sensation requires the five sense organs: eyes, ears, nose, tongue, and skin. It also includes the nerves that give us position sense, and our sense of movement. Think about the process of perceiving beauty around you.

— *Expression.* This is the process by which we communicate with and influence the world. The body parts involved include the muscles, ligaments, tendons, and bones. This includes the facial muscles and the muscles of the vocal cords. The brain is also involved as it directs these body parts. Think about the process of connecting with the world around you.

— *Regulation.* This is the process by which your body coordinates all its other activities. It involves the whole nervous system, including the parts of the nervous system that regulate autonomic functions, such as blood pressure, gastric movements, heart rate, and resting muscle tone. It also includes the glands that secrete hormones: pituitary, hypothalamus, thyroid, adrenals, and sex organs. Think about all the cells in your body communicating with one another.

BRIAN'S RESULTS FROM INNER HARMONY PRACTICE

Brian has worked with Inner Harmony over the last two weeks, but he still feels it is too much work to think about each of the processes in detail. He has taken his teacher's advice and just thinks briefly about each process and then returns to concentrating on the sense of appreciation and gratitude for his body. This is increasing his sense of peace with himself and is lowering his ongoing stress level.

MARIA'S RESULTS FROM INNER HARMONY PRACTICE

After one month of practicing Inner Harmony twice per week, Maria realizes that her breathing has naturally become smoother. As her breathing has become smoother, she finds her physical movements becoming more coordinated as well. Maria is now able to catch her headaches coming before her head actually starts hurting. This helps her to stop them effectively, either by doing a brief relaxation exercise or by taking her medication sooner.

Maria has also discovered that if she focuses on appreciation and gratitude and thinks about the process of digestion after eating, then she feels more satisfied with less food and her abdomen feels more comfortable.

HEALTH APPLICATION 3: HEALING LIGHT

Healing Light is the third health application. Many traditions speak of the healing properties of light. Healers often speak about seeing certain patterns of light when they work with people. Matter can be thought of as condensed light. So light is a powerful healing image that is also connected to your physical form.

When you do this exercise, you will be using your attending, concentrating, and opening skills to evoke an experience of a healing light. You will then bring the image of this light into your body so that you can experience the idea of good health on a deep physical level.

You must begin by remembering your intention. Your intention tells your mind what to create and gives coherence to the experiences your mind will produce.

After remembering your intention, concentrate on the idea of good health. Concentrating on the idea of good health enables you to experience that idea. As you concentrate on the idea of good health, you identify and disengage from any particular images that arise. Eventually the images begin to dissolve into an experience of light or colors. The light is what you work with, because it will contain all the images and bring their positive energy into your body.

BRIAN'S FIRST EXPERIENCE WITH HEALING LIGHT

Brian has practiced Inner Harmony enough that he can now feel love and gratitude for his body. He is ready to move on to the next technique, Healing Light.

Brian starts by lying down and covering himself with a blanket. **"The Healing Light application can create a very altered state of consciousness. It helps if you practice lying down so that you can completely let go."** He then remembers his intention by remembering his goals for meditation and his goal for this session: experiencing a deep sense of health and healing.

Brian has been practicing so often that as he does these things, his body is already settling down. After a couple of easy breaths, he is quite relaxed. He centers on the thought "My face is soft and gentle" for a couple of minutes and then concentrates on the feeling of appreciation and gratitude for his body. As he feels his body respond to that, Brian moves into the practice of Healing Light.

Brian concentrates on the idea of excellent health. As he does so, he realizes he doesn't have a clear idea of what that means. As his mind starts to feel confused he remembers his teacher saying, **"Getting a clear idea of excellent health can be difficult. It can help to think about the results of excellent health: how your body would feel, how easy it would be to breathe, how your heart would be strong, how your whole body would be vibrant and all the cells in it would be alive."** Brian remembers various events from his life—playing basketball with friends, swimming in the ocean, hiking in the mountains. His mind moves from one to another. He remembers feeling strong and flexible, being able to breathe deeply and easily with his heart pumping strongly. Brian suddenly realizes he is feeling somewhat regretful. He misses the way he used to feel. **"Remember that you are using the memory simply to evoke the idea of excellent health. If you have other thoughts or emotions come up, simply identify them, disengage from them, and return your concentration to the sense of feeling healthy. If this is too difficult, then return to practicing the exercise you started with, Autonomic Relaxation or Inner Harmony."**

Brian identifies his feeling as regret and goes back to concentrating on the body sensations of feeling healthy. He remembers his experiences with Autonomic Relaxation and how good that exercise felt. Brian relaxes more and more, and his thoughts become more positive. He thinks about how good he feels and how he enjoys the health he has.

As he concentrates more and more on the internal sensations of feeling healthy, images start to come to mind. He sees an eagle flying through the air, then the face of a wolf appears. He sees runners competing in a race, and he hears the sound of the ocean. **"As you focus your mind on the idea of excellent health, it will often produce imagined experiences. They are representations of your experiences of health in a symbolic manner. In this exercise you will move to a level beneath the symbols, so avoid analyzing these images. Just notice them in an accepting manner, then let them go and return to the feeling of health."**

Brian disengages from the images and returns to concentrating on the idea of health. As he does so, the images gradually fade. Soon everything seems to be getting dark. Brian waits for a bit, but nothing appears. He wonders if he has done something wrong. **"After the images fade, there is often a period of darkness. Remember that your intention at the beginning of the session was to experience a healing light and wait for what appears. Sometimes people experience the healing light as darkness. As long as you stay connected with the idea of health and are feeling peaceful, you are doing OK."**

Brian continues to concentrate on the feeling of health and remembers his intention to experience a healing light. At first more images appear, but they pass as he disengages from them. Soon he is experiencing just a variety of colors in various shapes. He continues to concentrate on the idea of health while he watches the colors in his mind's eye.

Brian suddenly finds himself aware of a bright yellow light that fills his whole inner vision. He remembers someone saying that white light is for healing, and then someone else saying that green represents health. He begins to get worried that he is using the wrong color. **"Accept the color your mind gives you. There are no absolute rules about what colors to use. Everyone is unique. You may experience any color or combination of colors. The colors may change when you repeat the exercise. Just concentrate on the idea of**

health and allow your mind to create the color it wants to use for the occasion."

Reassured, Brian pays attention to the yellow light. It feels warm and comforting and seems to resonate with the feeling of health he was experiencing. He lets go of concentrating on the feeling of health and opens to the yellow light. He remembers the feeling of vastness he experienced during the opening exercises and feels space inside himself. As he does this, he imagines the yellow light flowing into that space completely.

Brian imagines the light filling his head, neck, shoulders, arms, chest, abdomen, pelvis, and legs. He allows himself to feel more and more space inside himself, and imagines the yellow light filling it. Soon he is feeling the yellow light as a warm, physical, healing substance inside him.

As he continues to concentrate on the yellow light while feeling the space inside him, he loses track of his body's size and shape. He feels like he has become a ball of yellow light that is swirling and moving in beautiful patterns. He enjoys the experience, remembering his intention of good health every now and then.

After his watch alarm beeps to signal the end of the session, Brian reflects on how peaceful the experience was. He appreciates how his mind was able to create the image of light once he trusted it. He then reorients to time and place by remembering his physical surroundings. He then reorients to his body by wiggling his fingers and toes and then flexing and stretching his arms and legs for a few seconds before opening his eyes.

MARIA'S FIRST EXPERIENCE WITH HEALING LIGHT

Maria is starting her first session with the Healing Light technique. She remembers her intention and then goes rapidly through the Inner Harmony technique. This takes her about five minutes and she feels peaceful and relaxed. Maria then concentrates on the idea of excellent health. She experiences a feeling of vibrancy and energy in her body. She imagines being bouncy and vivacious, enjoying life and having plenty of energy to accomplish the day's tasks.

As Maria does this, she feels more and more comfortable. She remembers that her intention for the session was to experience a healing light. A series of images appears and disappears. She stays disengaged from thoughts and images, and feels as if she is floating peacefully. Maria recalls her intention to experience a healing light and then remembers the sense of expansion and contraction she felt when she did opening practice. Soon she feels the familiar space and vastness inside her body. She remembers her intention to experience a healing light. Suddenly she is aware of a blue light inside her. As she notices it, it changes to yellow, then green, then red, and then back to blue. Then a yellow stripe appears followed by some green swirls. Maria remembers, **"The color of the light does not really matter. It is OK if the color changes or if there are several colors at once. Remember your intention every now and then and continue to experience the vastness and space, letting the colors do what they want."**

Maria disengages from trying to stabilize the colors and just enjoys the experience. The colors continue to flow and change, and this seems to enhance the experience of openness. She feels as if her whole body is a huge, rainbow-colored ball. After enjoying this for a while, Maria realizes that her alarm is beeping. It is time to finish. She reflects on how remembering her intention and then letting go aided her in having a very enjoyable experience. She then reorients to time and place, wiggles her fingers and toes, flexes her arms and legs, and takes a deep breath before she opens her eyes.

INSTRUCTIONS FOR HEALTH APPLICATION 3: HEALING LIGHT

- This application uses attending, concentrating, and opening skills. The exercise can take between twenty and forty-five minutes to complete, so set aside at least thirty minutes.
- Start by sitting or lying in a comfortable position in which you can relax completely. Be sure you are warm.
- Remember your intention to experience a feeling of health as deeply as possible.
- Concentrate on the idea of *excellent* health. One way of doing this is to remember a time when you felt great and that your whole body was in optimal shape. Another way is to think about what excellent health would feel like. Use your concentration skills to increase the strength of this feeling. The goal of this step is to experience the idea of excellent health as clearly as possible.
- If specific memories or images come, identify and disengage from them. Continue to concentrate on the idea of excellent health.
- Once you feel a connection with the idea of excellent health, pay attention to any colors that are appearing. If you are having images or memories, pay attention to the colors in the images. If your visual field is dark, just wait expectantly.
- Ask your mind to create a color that represents the idea of excellent health that you are feeling. Continue to concentrate on the feeling of health while just watching the colors that appear. Trust your mind to create the color(s) that are right for you. Remember that black is a color too, and it may be the right one for you.
- Now open to that healing light. Remember the sense of vastness from opening practice and allow that healing light to fill it. Let go of concentrating on the idea of excellent health and

concentrate on the image of light while experiencing the vastness.

- Imagine the light filling your whole body. Your body may feel like it has changed size or shape. That does not matter, just allow the light to fill everywhere that feels like you. Imagine the light filling this space fully.
- Continue to experience the light flowing and moving through the space. Every now and then remember your intention to have excellent health.
- You may lose track of your usual body dimensions and you may lose track of time. When you finish the session, reflect on your experience and then reorient yourself gradually to time, place, and your body.

BRIAN'S RESULTS FROM HEALING LIGHT PRACTICE

Brian practices the Healing Light exercise once per week for the next month. He also practices Autonomic Relaxation once per week. He rotates through the basic exercises of attending, concentrating, and opening during the other sessions.

At the end of the month, his wife points out to him that he has made some positive changes in his diet. He is eating smaller portions and is skipping dessert frequently. When he hears that, Brian suddenly realizes that he has not been eating the doughnuts at work during the Friday morning meeting either. He is amazed that he has made these changes without even trying. It is like his mind is automatically acting in accord with the intention for better health that he focuses on at the beginning of the Healing Light technique. When he goes in for his scheduled doctor's visit a couple of days later, he is pleasantly surprised to find that he has lost several pounds and that his blood pressure has decreased slightly.

MARIA'S RESULTS FROM HEALING LIGHT PRACTICE

Over the next three weeks, Maria practices Inner Harmony and Healing Light once per week each, and practices the basic attending, concentrating, and opening techniques once. At the end of that time she notices that she is taking life a lot more easily. She is not as insistent about keeping things in order. This more easygoing attitude has coincided with an almost complete elimination of her headaches. About this her teacher said, **"It is common for illnesses to be made worse by things that are not directly related to the disease process: lifestyle, emotions, behaviors, or attitudes. It is hard to discover those indirect causes by thinking about the disease directly. When you try, you sometimes come up with too many possible indirect causes. By using the mental quality of spaciousness, the Healing Light technique allows your mind to find and change those things that are truly related to the illness, directly or indirectly. That naturally leads to improvement."**

REVIEW OF HEALTH APPLICATIONS

As you practice these applications, your body will be more resistant to the pressures of our fast-paced world. It will feel more peaceful and coherent. You will feel healthier, more energetic, and more comfortable.

The three applications use different mental abilities and have somewhat different effects. Autonomic Relaxation uses centering and attending skills to create a deep state of relaxation that allows your body to heal faster and recover from fatigue. Inner Harmony uses attending and concentrating skills to create a positive relationship between yourself and your body. It counters the common messages received from yourself and others that your body is defective. You can experience your body as wonderful, even if it is not flawless. The last exercise, Healing Light, uses attending, concentrating, and opening skills to evoke an altered state of consciousness that can create healing in indirect ways.

When you practice these, you should get familiar enough with Autonomic Relaxation to be able to do it easily and quickly before moving to Inner Harmony. Once you can do the Autonomic Relaxation and become relaxed in five minutes or less, you are ready to move to Inner Harmony. You can then practice Autonomic Relaxation as a brief technique.

As you get more skill with Inner Harmony, you will be able to move through that application more quickly as well. Then you can use it, too, as a brief technique several times a day, thereby maintaining a positive attitude toward your body.

Once you can consistently experience that positive attitude toward your body during the Inner Harmony exercise, you are ready to move to Healing Light. Practice the Healing Light exercise one or two times per week. You can practice Autonomic Relaxation or Inner Harmony in one or two extended sessions per week as well.

It usually takes one or two months to experience success with each of these applications. When you move on to another set of applications, you can maintain your health gains by continuing to practice brief versions of Autonomic Relaxation or Inner Harmony a couple of times during the day.

If you want to focus on health applications, then you can do so on a three-week cycle. Practice the extended attending, extended concentrating, and extended opening exercises for thirty minutes each during the three weeks in order to maintain your basic skills. Then use the rest of your extended sessions to practice one or more of the extended health applications. Continue to do the brief practices for attending, concentrating, and opening as well as a brief health application several times per day.

8 performance: enhancing your skills and your energy

WHEN YOU USE meditation to enhance your performance, you take a big step toward finding peace amid the pressures of modern life. You learn to increase your abilities by staying calm when pressure builds. You can use visualization so that your unconscious mind can work on several tasks at once. And you are able to get past blocks so that you can stop spinning your wheels and move forward.

Meditation literature is full of stories about people who have used meditation to enhance their performance. Many athletes use meditation to improve their skills, and many of our students have used it to help them do better both at work and on the playing field. You, too, can use meditation to increase your performance at physical and mental tasks.

Physical performance is just one aspect of performance that is enhanced by meditation. Mental performance can be increased as well. And of course, work performance in today's world is more associated with mental skills than it is with physical ability. By increasing your mental performance you will improve your effectiveness and efficiency at work.

The basic exercises you have been practicing develop memory, concentration, flexible thinking, abstract reasoning, and creativity. These mental skills will be augmented by meditation applications. There are several ways to enhance performance using meditation. You will learn three applications, each of which will enhance your performance in a different manner. The first application, Heightened Focus, enables you to maintain an alert and calm state, even under pressure. If you are too anxious while doing a task, your performance will suffer and you will use more energy than you need to. If you are too relaxed while doing a task, you will not be energized enough to do well. Meditation helps you be energized for the task while staying calm and unstressed. This is taught in the Heightened Focus application.

Meditation also helps you by improving your imagination, as you will learn in the second application, Directed Imagination. Your imagination is in fact so powerful that if you vividly imagine doing something well, your mind can learn from the experience as though you had actually performed the task. This is called mental rehearsal, or visualization. Meditation improves your ability to visualize, and increases the power of the visualizations. After you have learned Directed Imagination, you will be able to practice visualizing without having to concentrate on the process. You will be able to visualize a successful result even while doing other tasks.

Finally, many people have internal blocks that keep them from succeeding. These obstacles can come from negative programming, fears about what success will lead to, or from pursuing goals that are destructive for them. The third application, Clearing Blocks, will teach you to move around obstacles, or to recognize when they exist because you are pursuing inappropriate goals.

PERFORMANCE APPLICATION 1: HEIGHTENED FOCUS

Imagine being totally focused on your task and feeling so calm that your performance is effortless. That is what Heightened Focus will enable you to experience. In order to do well under pressure, you have to be highly alert and calm at the same time.

Many people become more nervous as they get more alert, and they get less alert when they become calm. By learning to become extremely alert and focused while staying calm, you can bring more energy to your task in a coherent manner.

This technique uses your centering and attending skills to help you stay focused on your task while disengaging from things that distract you. When you are absorbed in a task, you are not aware of distractions, and your energy is completely devoted to performing the task. Some people describe this state as being "in the zone."

When you are in that focused, calm state, your body and mind work much more efficiently, allowing you to accomplish far more with less energy. This helps you remain peaceful because you are meeting your responsibilities more easily. The experience can even generate energy so that you complete a task feeling more energized than when you started.

The technique, Heightened Focus, is something you do while engaged in the task. It is not to be done in extended sessions away from the event you want to work on. To do the technique, center your awareness on something that is centrally related to your task. You maintain a continuous awareness of that aspect of the task while staying peripherally aware of your surroundings. You then identify and disengage from any thoughts, sensations, or emotions that hinder you in completing the task. This uses centering and attending skills to focus your awareness to a higher state.

Knowing what to choose as a center can be tricky. You need to find something that is related to your task and that will not distract you. If you were playing tennis, you might center on the ball. If you were running, you could center on the image of the finish, or a feeling of strength in your legs. If you were writing, you would center on the points that you wanted to make, or the idea you wanted to convey.

Once you have chosen something to center on, you should maintain a continuous awareness of it. If anything distracts you, identify it. The distractions are often thoughts, but they can be sensations or emotions as well. If the distraction is helpful, integrate it into your awareness. If not, then disengage from it and go back to your original center. For example, if you were playing tennis and noticed that your opponent had moved out of position on the court, this would be a helpful observation. If, however, you were distracted by thoughts about not doing well, then these thoughts would be unhelpful and you would disengage from them and return to centering your awareness on the ball. As you practice, your mind will learn to automatically avoid unhelpful distractions and increase its awareness of those things that are helpful.

BRIAN'S FIRST EXPERIENCE WITH HEIGHTENED FOCUS

Brian's performance goal was to improve his golf game. He has noticed some improvement from practicing the basic exercises, but he wants to do better. He knows that he tends to tense up when he is making a shot, and he hopes that practicing Heightened Focus can reduce this.

The next time he tees off, he centers on the golf ball. As he looks at it, he keeps his mind alert. Suddenly he is aware of a number of thoughts that were previously hidden. "Wonder if you'll drive it short. Don't slice it off to the left. Watch out for the water trap." His mind feels like an overly concerned parent giving him unneeded advice. Brian identifies these thoughts as unhelpful distractions. Because of his experience with attending meditation, he is able to disengage from them and center again on the ball.

As he maintains his focus on the ball, he notices an increasing number of body sensations. He can feel how his weight is balanced on his feet. He can sense the position of his hips and shoulders in relation to the club more clearly than before. He identifies these as helpful, and by noticing them while maintaining awareness of the ball, he feels his alertness increase. He is more and more aware of his body, the ball, and the relationship between them. Brian is then aware of how his golf partner is looking at him. He identifies this as an unhelpful distraction and disengages from it, refocusing on the ball.

As Brian disengages from the distractions, he feels like he has more energy focused on hitting the ball. His energy feels coherent and not as scattered. The club seems to swing forward on its own without much effort, and the ball takes off from the tee.

Brian continues to use this technique while he plays the next eight holes. Sometimes he feels like he is straining to maintain his focus on the ball. He remembers, **"Maintain a gentle focus on the ball. You are to center on the ball. That means your focus is gentle, not too intense. You get a gentle focus not by concentrating harder on the ball but by disengaging from distractions. That way the only things you are paying attention to are sensations, thoughts, and emotions that are related to your task."** Brian has a few instances when he feels this happen. It is an experience of being totally focused, not just on the ball but on everything related to hitting it. The rest of the world seems to disappear.

Brian notices that when he has this calm and alert focus, the ball goes farther and straighter than it usually does. He starts straining to make that happen and his shots get worse. **"Do not strain to increase your performance. The key is to disengage from things that are distracting you. The desire to make the technique work is a powerful distraction, so disengage from that too. Accept the fact that it takes practice to become more consistent."** Brian remembers to be patient with himself and not try to make a huge improvement overnight.

MARIA'S FIRST EXPERIENCE WITH HEIGHTENED FOCUS

Maria's performance goal is to improve her presentations at work. While she has become calmer throughout much of the day because of practicing the basic exercises, she still gets nervous giving presentations. She either forgets some of the points she wants to make or she becomes so focused on them that she presents in a rapid, flustered style that can confuse her audience. Maria wasn't sure how to practice the technique before she actually gave the presentation. Her teacher advised, **"You could give some trial presentations and practice the technique then, but it would be better to use the technique in a situation that occurs more frequently. Are there any situations in which you feel the same way, tense and flustered about saying something in front of others?"**

Maria realizes that she feels this way when she makes comments or asks questions in a meeting. She decides that she can practice the Heightened Focus technique when she asks questions in meetings so that she will be familiar with it and able to use it when she makes presentations.

In the next meeting, Maria wants to ask a question and feels the familiar tension come up. She centers on the question, keeping her awareness on it. At the same time, she attends to what is distracting her and disengages from it. At first she feels tightness in her stomach and weakness in her legs. As she disengages from these and goes back to centering on the question, she notices a number of thoughts that she had been unaware of. Part of her mind is thinking, "That's a stupid question. People will think you are really dumb."

These thoughts are hard to disengage from, so Maria identifies the activity her mind is doing as "criticizing." Identifying the process helps her to disengage from the thoughts and return to centering on the question she wants to ask.

This process has taken a few seconds, and now that the distractions are less, Maria is more aware of other people and the comments they are making. She feels more present in the room and understands how her question is about a point that other people are having difficulty understanding too. As she speaks out, she notices that her tone of voice is firmer and her body feels stronger than it usually does. The speaker responds politely to her question, and Maria feels pleased by the experience.

INSTRUCTIONS FOR PERFORMANCE APPLICATION 1: HEIGHTENED FOCUS

- This application is to be done during the event or performance in which you'd like to see improvement.
- Remember your intention. Get a clear idea of what you want to improve, and set that as your goal.
- Center on something central to succeeding at your immediate task.
- Finding the appropriate thing to center on can be difficult. Trial and error may be necessary. Here are some suggestions:

— In sports such as golf or tennis, center on the ball.

— In endurance sports such as swimming or running, center on the image of the finish, or on the image of being full of energy.

— When taking a test, center on each question in turn.

— While giving a talk or writing, center on the major points you want to make.

- Maintain continuous awareness of your center.
- Attend to thoughts, sensations, or emotions that arise. If they are helpful, incorporate them into your awareness. If they are unhelpful, disengage from them and bring your awareness back to your center. Continue this as long as you are not straining.
- After the event, recall your experience and note any patterns in the distracting thoughts or sensations.

BRIAN'S AND MARIA'S RESULTS FROM HEIGHTENED FOCUS PRACTICE

After a couple of weeks, Brian is able to consistently feel the positive results of Heightened Focus practice. He feels more energized and relaxed after a round of golf. He has also lowered his handicap by a couple of strokes. He is not sure if this will continue, and sometimes he wonders if it is just luck. But he is enjoying the game more and is less critical of himself.

After using the Heightened Focus technique during several meetings, Maria notices that she is naturally feeling more confident when speaking in front of others. She has a presentation coming up in three weeks and hopes that this and the next meditation application will make a big difference.

PERFORMANCE APPLICATION 2: DIRECTED IMAGINATION

Your imagination is so powerful that if you imagine something vividly enough, you can experience it as a real event. For example, if you imagine washing your hands in warm water, your hands will warm up. This ability of your imagination allows you to use it to improve your performance. If you vividly imagine successful performances, your mind will learn from them just as if they had occurred. As far as your mind is concerned, the events did occur.

This technique is often called visualization. We do not like that term because it restricts your imagination to imagined visual experiences. Many people imagine sounds, movements, or feelings better than they do visual images. You do not need to have a visual experience or a visual learning style in order to use this technique.

The technique, Directed Imagination, uses attending and concentrating skills. The concentrating skills are especially important. Since you have practiced the basic concentrating exercise, you will be able to direct your imagination in the correct manner without straining it. The brief concentration exercise you have been practicing, in which you remember an event from earlier in the day, is also helpful. It has taught you to imagine in all sensory modalities and to do so quickly.

Directed Imagination has two versions: extended and brief. During the extended sessions, you will be vividly imagining a successful performance. In the brief sessions, you will condense that successful imagination into a few seconds, and recall it frequently throughout the day. That will enable your mind to keep training while you do other tasks.

The most important point with Directed Imagination is that you have to imagine *success*. If you imagine a different result, then you will not train your mind to be successful. That seems obvious, but we have worked with people who were not precise about what they imagined. Their images had elements of failure in them, so the technique did not work as well.

That is why the concentrating and attending skills you've developed are so crucial to this technique. Concentration allows you to vividly imagine the experience. Your attending skills will allow you to identify and disengage from any elements of the image that are not consistent with the successful result you want to imagine.

BRIAN'S FIRST EXPERIENCE WITH DIRECTED IMAGINATION

Brian knows that he could improve his golf game significantly by putting more consistently and accurately. He wants to use Directed Imagination to improve his putting. His teacher advises, **"Imagine putting the golf ball successfully. You may see yourself doing that in your mind's eye, but you want to use your other senses as well. Imagine the sounds, the smells, the feel of the club in your hands, and the position and movement of your body. You can connect to the image of putting well by remembering a couple of successful putts. This is similar to using the brief concentration technique."**

Brian begins the extended session by sitting comfortably and focusing his intention to putt more accurately. He relaxes and remembers standing on the green holding the putter and looking at the ball. The image of the green takes a few minutes to develop, almost as if it were a photograph. Brian reexperiences bits and pieces of the scene. He sees the ball and the grass, he feels the warm sun on his back. He smells the clean air and feels the touch of the light breeze. He feels the roughness of the putter's handle on his palms and feels the weight of it in his hands. He imagines swinging the club and sees the ball roll smoothly and come to rest just to the left of the cup. He identifies this as an unsuccessful result, and disengages from it by returning his awareness to the image before he hit the ball. He then imagines hitting the ball again, and again it misses the cup. Brian feels frustrated. How is he going to use this technique when he can't imagine success? **"If you try to imagine success and you experience failure in the image, you may be trying to imagine something too difficult at this time. Simply imagine success at something easier and work up to imagining success at more difficult actions."**

Brian realizes that he was trying to imagine a successful putt that would be one of the longest putts he has ever made. He changes the image so that he is only a couple of feet from the cup. This time it is easy to imagine the ball going into the cup. After doing this a couple of times, he begins to imagine putting from different positions on the green. If the ball does not go into the cup, then he imagines putting from a closer position. When Brian reflects on the experience after the session, he realizes that he was gradually able to make longer putts in his imagination. Brian realizes he can do this in a brief session by imagining doing just one successful putt from a close distance.

MARIA'S FIRST EXPERIENCE WITH DIRECTED IMAGINATION

Maria has a presentation coming up in three weeks. She now feels more comfortable speaking up at meetings after practicing the Heightened Focus application, but she knows she won't be able to give her talk without feeling agitated. Maria knows that giving a mock presentation can help. She realizes that she can use Directed Imagination to imagine giving her talk, and that that will enable her to practice it many times before she has to give it.

Maria sits down for her session of Directed Imagination and remembers her intention to give the talk calmly and clearly. After relaxing for a couple of minutes, she imagines that she is starting her talk. She concentrates on the things she wants to say and imagines that she is standing in front of the audience beginning her presentation. The image that appears is muddled. As Maria struggles to clarify it, she realizes that she is not absolutely sure of what she wants to say. This astonishes her because she thought she knew what points she wanted to make. She remembers, **"When using Directed Imagination, it will be difficult if your idea of what you want to accomplish is vague or incomplete. Concentrate on what you want to accomplish until you have a clear idea of that. That may take a couple of sessions. Only after you have a clear image of success are you to use Directed Imagination."**

Maria focuses on the ideas she wants to present. She attends to other ideas that come to mind. She continues to do this for the next few minutes. Suddenly she sees how some of the ideas she wants to present do not fit in with the main point of her presentation. She also realizes she has some new ideas that will fit with the main point and demonstrate it more clearly. She reflects on this and then gets a pen and paper to write these new ideas down. After writing them down, she restarts the Directed Imagination exercise. This time she is able to get a clear image of giving the presentation. She notices that she is able to imagine delivering the points she wants to make in a clear and calm manner, without anxiety.

After giving the imagined talk, Maria reflects on her experience. She reviews the highlights of the presentation and considers how the exercise forced her to clarify her objectives. She realizes she can do a brief version of the exercise in which she imagines delivering the main points of the talk.

INSTRUCTIONS FOR PERFORMANCE APPLICATION 2: DIRECTED IMAGINATION

- Reflect on the fact that Directed Imagination combines concentrating, attending, and centering.
- It is important that you not choose goals that involve comparisons with others. For example, setting a personal record in an event is an acceptable goal. Beating everyone else in the event is not. While one can successfully visualize winning awards, we believe that caution is necessary. If two people visualize winning the same award, then conflict is inevitable. Inner peace is not found by becoming more competitive.
- Sit or lie in a comfortable position in which you can completely relax.
- Start by focusing your intention on achieving your goal.
- Center on achieving the desired result or goal. This may be more of an idea than a concrete event.
- Attend to thoughts, sensations, and emotions that arise. Make sure you are aware of the emotions that are connected to achieving your goal. Continue this process until you can vividly imagine the experience of achieving your goal.
- Now concentrate on that experience until you are absorbed in it. Make sure you imagine the emotions as well as the sights, sounds, and other sensory experiences.
- As you end your concentration, reflect on any ideas that come to mind.
- Develop a brief version of the exercise in which you imagine the highlights of the successful experience. Then practice the brief version frequently each day.

BRIAN'S AND MARIA'S RESULTS FROM DIRECTED IMAGINATION PRACTICE

Brian has practiced the extended version of Directed Imagination for about four weeks. He can consistently imagine successful putts. He has also practiced the brief version a couple of times per day. The combination of the two has caused him to imagine successful putts even while he is not thinking about golf. These will occur while he is walking or driving or taking a shower.

The results have been pleasing. Brian's increased confidence at putting has helped him be more relaxed during his approach shots. Since he is more relaxed on those shots, they are more accurate. His putts are more accurate as well. He has taken five strokes off his handicap in the last month.

Maria used Directed Imagination diligently during the three weeks before her presentation. She used the extended version twice per week, and she practiced a brief version several times each day. Within a couple of days of starting the exercise, she found that she was having ideas for improving the talk spontaneously. She started carrying a notepad with her to jot them down. Her imagined presentation became clearer and more coherent.

When she gave the talk, it was much easier than usual. She was still anxious before it began, but once she started, the imagined practice sessions carried her through. She was able to make each of her points in a calm, unhurried manner. She also answered questions without getting flustered.

PERFORMANCE APPLICATION 3: CLEARING BLOCKS

Goal-oriented visualization can be very useful at helping us succeed. However, sometimes we have unconscious mental blocks—negative or positive—that get in the way of success. Negative blocks keep us from using our skills and abilities in a fulfilling manner. Negative blocks are often related to unconscious fears of failure. They can also come from emotionally painful experiences. Negative blocks need to be overcome so that we can move on.

It may seem strange, but sometimes blocks are good for us. Positive blocks keep us from achieving successes that we are attracted to but that would cause trouble for us. For example, we may want to make more money, but we're afraid that it would harm our family relationships. Sometimes we think we know what we want, but a deeper, inner self knows better. Our inner self then puts up one obstacle after another. The goal becomes more and more difficult to reach. Many people have spent a lot of energy chasing goals that they later found to be meaningless. Positive blocks are warnings that we are trying to go in a direction that is not good for us. They need to be listened to so that we can move in a healthy direction.

Clearing Blocks is for people who feel that something internal is getting in the way of their success. It is also for people who may be uneasy about the goals they are pursuing. Clearing Blocks is definitely required when Directed Imagination does not succeed or has only partial success.

BRIAN'S FIRST EXPERIENCE WITH CLEARING BLOCKS

Brian is very pleased with how Directed Imagination and Heightened Focus have improved his golf game. He has taken five strokes off his handicap in the last month. Several of his playing buddies are impressed by his improvement. He wants to keep getting better and is thinking a lot about how he can improve even more. He is considering new golf clubs and wants to increase his visualization practice. Golf is on his mind more than ever.

After a few days Brian notices that he can't seem to do the Directed Imagination exercise any more. The images waver, and he can't imagine successful putts, even if he tries making them a couple of feet from the cup. His efforts to continue the technique just seem to cause strain. When he asks his teacher about this, the response is, **"It sounds like your mind is telling you it doesn't want to do that technique. There may be a good reason for that. Practice the Clearing Blocks technique to find out what your mind is having difficulty with."**

Brian sits down for the session. He remembers his intention is to improve his golf game. He imagines himself on the golf course, and after the image becomes clear, he does an opening technique. He imagines being on a high mountain and that the scene from the golf course is far below him. He feels peaceful and content as he experiences the vastness of the mountain. As he imagines the golf course far below him, he remembers his intention is to improve his golf game. Brian notices that something is disturbing the peace he feels. As he attends to it, he identifies it as uneasiness, as if something is not quite right. He notices that this feeling increases if he observes the scene of the golf course. He remembers his intention to improve his golf game again.

Suddenly Brian hears the words "What will that get me?" As he imagines looking down on the golf course again, the words repeat: "What will that get me?" Brian sees other images coming into view. He attends to these and identifies them as his wife, his children, his house, and his job. He realizes that his golf game was becoming an obsession for him. If he had continued, he would have been spending more and more time and money on it. This time and money would be better used elsewhere. He realizes that continuing to focus so much energy on his golf game would have a negative impact on his job and on his family life and that it is not worth it.

From his imagined position high on the mountain, Brian can see golf in perspective. It is just a hobby for him and its purpose is to help him have fun and relax. He is not a professional golfer, and he can be content with that. Brian feels a sense of relief, like something that was squeezing his mind has loosened its grasp. He reviews the insights he has gained from the session and then reorients to time and place before opening his eyes.

MARIA'S FIRST EXPERIENCE WITH CLEARING BLOCKS

Maria has been pleased with the success of Directed Imagination. She is much less anxious when giving presentations. However, there are still occasions when she feels tension in her stomach and weakness in her legs. These occur as she starts her talk and at random intervals throughout it. The episodes last only a few seconds, but they are distressing. Maria has not been able to eliminate these with Directed Imagination. She decides to use the Clearing Blocks technique.

Maria starts by remembering her intention to understand why she is still feeling bursts of anxiety when giving presentations. She focuses on the image of herself giving a talk, and she repeats her intention to herself. Maria then goes through the opening technique she enjoys by imagining her body is expanding and contracting as she breathes. She has practiced this enough so that her mind responds quickly. Soon she feels like she is drifting peacefully. **"Remember your intention every now and then to keep your mind oriented. If you only enjoy the peace, you may not get the information you want."** Maria remembers the reason she is doing this, and sees herself standing at the front of a room giving a talk. As she watches, the scene seems to get more distant, like she is floating away from it. She remembers her intention again, and the scene drifts closer. This sequence repeats itself a couple of times. Suddenly Maria realizes that the scene has changed. As she attends to the details, she notices that she is much younger and that the room is a classroom.

Maria feels sad and anxious as she notices these details. She identifies the emotions, and disengages from them by focusing on the expansion and contraction. As Maria watches the scene, she remembers having to give an oral report in the fifth grade. She remembers getting ready to speak and then having an attack of stage fright and forgetting everything she was going to say. It was very embarrassing; several of her classmates laughed, and she felt like running away and never coming back. She was unable to give the report. What hurt the most was that she had worked hard on the report, but her teacher blamed her stage fright on her not being prepared. She felt shame and hurt at her teacher's scolding. The experience had been forgotten, but the shame and hurt continued to affect her for years.

As Maria remembers this, the hurt and fear seem to arise and then dissipate in the spaciousness. She watches this happen and then can remember the event without much reaction. It happened, it was uncomfortable, she was misunderstood, and now she can move beyond that. Maria reflects on that realization and then ends the session by reorienting to time and place and then opening her eyes.

INSTRUCTIONS FOR PERFORMANCE APPLICATION 3: CLEARING BLOCKS

- Sometimes a goal seems elusive, or it seems that something is blocking us from that goal. This can occur in spite of using Directed Imagination. A different approach is needed when this happens.
- Directed Imagination uses concentration to generate a laser-like focus on succeeding. Clearing Blocks uses opening and spaciousness to pull back from the goal and see what might be causing the difficulties.
- Start by sitting or lying in a comfortable position.
- Remember your intention to understand how to resolve the blocks to attaining your goal.
- Center on the image of achieving the goal. Attend to thoughts, emotions, and sensations that arise.
- Use an opening technique to pull back mentally from that image. For example, imagine being on a mountaintop and seeing the image of the goal farther and farther below you.
- Notice what ideas or images come to mind. Stay alert for any that seem to be opposed to achieving the goal.
- Restate your intention a couple of times and continue to apply the opening technique. For example, continue to imagine yourself on the mountaintop and see things far below you.
- As you come out of the meditation, reflect on the ideas and images that came up and take notes on any that seem relevant or surprising.

This exercise is essentially the opposite of Directed Imagination. In Directed Imagination, you center on the goal, allow it to develop by attending, and then focus your awareness using concentration. In Clearing Blocks, you center on the goal, allow it to develop by attending, and then *shift* your awareness by opening.

BRIAN'S AND MARIA'S RESULTS FROM CLEARING BLOCKS PRACTICE

After practicing the Clearing Blocks exercise, Brian feels much less intense about improving his golf game. He continues to use the brief visualization of successful putting every now and then. He also uses the Heightened Focus technique when he is playing golf. However, he realizes that there are more important things than golf. One of the most important of those is his family. He plans to start the relationship applications of meditation in his next session.

Maria has felt a real relief from doing the Clearing Blocks exercise. She now feels a lot easier about speaking out. The anxiety attacks do not occur during presentations anymore. All she feels is a mild discomfort as she gets ready to start speaking. She realizes this is excitement, not anxiety, and it actually gets her energized so that she can deliver a good talk. She is satisfied with the results of the performance applications and is looking forward to using the techniques for improving her relationships.

REVIEW OF PERFORMANCE APPLICATIONS

You now have a set of tools that will enable you to improve your performance in a large number of activities. You will improve while keeping a sense of efficiency and flow. You will feel less need to compete and will instead be able to simply act, letting the results take care of themselves. This will increase your sense of peace as you use your energy more coherently on tasks that are truly important to you.

As you practice the three applications, you will find that they complement one another. Heightened Focus enhances your awareness while performing an activity, and allows you to maintain a calm attitude as well. As you practice it, you will find that it becomes effortless. That state of effortless intensity and calm is sometimes referred to as "the zone" and is associated with peak performances.

Directed Imagination enables you to train your mind to experience success before the event occurs. It is important to imagine success, because you teach your mind what you imagine. As you get familiar with Directed Imagination, you will find that your mind is imagining success even while you are doing other activities that do not absorb your attention. That is the real power of the technique. Your mind does the practice automatically, without needing your attention.

The last application, Clearing Blocks, helps you not waste energy on pursuing goals that are not right for you. That way you can keep your use of Directed Imagination and Heightened Focus to activities that are best for you. Clearing Blocks also helps you overcome the inhibiting effects of negative experiences so that the first two exercises can work more effectively.

After you have completed this chapter and made progress toward enhancing your performance, you may be tempted to focus on another set of performance goals. However, we advise you to now work on applications from another chapter. There will always be more ways to improve your performance, but a peaceful life involves more than just being good at tasks. If you skipped over the health applications, go back to them, or move on to the applications for relationships and spirituality.

If you do want to focus on performance applications for a few weeks, then you can do so on a three-week cycle. Practice the extended attending, extended concentrating, and extended opening exercises for thirty minutes each during the three weeks in order to maintain your basic skills. Then use most of your extended sessions to practice the second performance application, Directed Imagination. Once in a while practice the third performance application, Clearing Blocks. Continue to do the brief practices for attending, concentrating, and opening as well as using Heightened Focus during the activity you are working to improve.

9 relationships: resolving conflict and reconnecting with your loved ones

INTERPERSONAL relationships can be an incredible source of peace and happiness. Unfortunately, they can also be a source of conflict and distress. Many people work hard to make their relationships more peaceful.

When we work on improving a relationship, we often fall into the trap of thinking the other person needs to understand us and change. We work hard to make the others understand us and to get them to change. However, we don't often *listen* to them. We don't hear them deeply. We want others to change without being willing to change ourselves.

Meditation techniques are effective tools for building our ability to listen and understand deeply. They have been shown to increase empathy in people who practice them. As our ability to empathize with others increases, we become more capable of changing our own behavior and being more compassionate.

The three applications presented in this chapter are effective tools for developing more peaceful relationships. The first application, Building Positive Energy, teaches you how to increase the sense of caring and affection in your relationships and avoid the "Where's my dinner?" trap (more on that below). The second, Closeness During Conflict, allows you to handle "hot" issues without losing touch with the other person. The third, Space Without Distance, allows you to experience a sense of personal space without having to become emotionally distant from others. Together these three applications increase your ability to understand the other person and make positive changes in the way you relate to him or her. These applications are described in a family setting, but they can be applied to relationships in any setting.

RELATIONSHIP APPLICATION 1: BUILDING POSITIVE ENERGY

There is a story about a young student who lived next door to a family with young children. The mother cooked for her husband and children and noticed that the student was quite poor. She felt it was little trouble to cook an extra portion for dinner and have one of her children take that to the student. For the first week, the student was quite thankful for receiving this free food. However, as the food kept coming day after day, the student's thanks became less and less audible. After several weeks, the mother had a very difficult day. All her children were sick and she was unable to cook dinner. Shortly after the usual dinnertime had come and gone she heard a knock on the door. When the harried mother opened it, she saw the student standing there. "Where's my dinner?" he asked.

This human tendency to take repeated kindness for granted has a destructive effect on relationships. All relationships have a balance of positive and negative aspects. There are things we really like about the other person, and there are things we could do without. Over time, the positive things are taken more and more for granted. They become less noticeable. Or they are only noticed when they're unexpectedly absent, as with the student's dinner. As we become less consciously aware of the positive elements of the relationship, the negative ones seem to grow larger. Usually they are not really getting that much bigger, it's only that the positive side of the relationship has become less obvious. We know intellectually that the other person is doing things for us, but we don't feel their effect.

Building Positive Energy is a meditation technique that restores your awareness of the positive side to your relationships. It helps you experience the other person in a more balanced manner, and restores your positive feelings for the things they do for you. To do the exercise, you center your awareness on the positive aspects of a given relationship by thinking and remembering about the kind and loving things the other person does for you. Sometimes the positive side is small and flickering. But even the embers of a loving relationship can be rekindled by reminding yourself of the positive things that are present.

BRIAN'S FIRST EXPERIENCE WITH BUILDING POSITIVE ENERGY

Brian begins his morning meditation session with the intention to improve his relationship with his teenage son. They quarrel often, and it seems they are always finding fault with each other. He has noticed some improvement since he began meditating several months ago. He would like to continue improving the relationship and do so more rapidly. He remembers his intention by thinking about this for a couple of minutes. Brian then centers on the sensations in his lower abdomen as he thinks "Calm – Relaxed" several times. After a few breaths he feels the familiar sense of calm. Brian then centers on some positive memories of his son. He does this by thinking about some good things his son has done and the positive feelings associated with them. As he does this, he starts to remember numerous negative things—his son's report card, messy room, clothing, hairstyle, and loud music come to mind. However, he identifies these and disengages from them, deliberately returning to centering on the positive things his son has done.

Nonetheless, Brian's irritation quickly returns. The memories of what he doesn't like about his son's behavior are entangling his mind. Brian struggles to return to his desired center, the positive memories, but he can't. **"Sometimes you will get caught by negative memories, and you won't be able to go directly back to the positive memories. When that happens, identify the emotions you are feeling and ignore the specific memories. Then go back to centering on your breath until you have disengaged from those negative emotions. Once you have done that, you are ready to return to centering on the positive memories."**

Brian identifies his emotions as anger and frustration. He then centers on the sensations in his lower abdomen, and in that way disengages from the emotions. The negative memories recede and, after a few breaths, he is able to think again about the positive aspects of the relationship with his son.

He notes that there are times when his son does speak respectfully to him. His son has also thanked him on a number of occasions. While his son's report card was not as good as Brian wanted it to be, there were a number of good grades on it.

When the session is over, Brian reflects on his experience. He realizes that there were a number of positive things he remembered that he hadn't before the exercise. He realizes that practicing this technique will help him keep a more balanced perspective on how his son is actually doing.

MARIA'S FIRST EXPERIENCE WITH BUILDING POSITIVE ENERGY

Maria has decided to spend some focused meditation time on improving the relationship she has with her husband. He has complained frequently about being nagged by her. As her self-awareness has increased since she began meditating, she has noticed that she does complain frequently. Her meditation practice has helped her reduce her complaints, but she feels that she needs to do something more definite about the problem.

Maria remembers her intention to improve the relationship, and specifically to center on the positive aspects of it during this session. Since she feels a little tense, she does the Autonomic Relaxation exercise for a couple of minutes, ending with the phrase "My face is soft and gentle." She then begins to think about the things her husband has done that are nice. At first she draws a blank, and thinks, "But he hasn't done anything really nice." She remembers her teacher's advice: **"When you look for positive things about your husband to center on, look for little things. Remember any smiles, any caresses, any times he did something helpful around the house. Think about how much effort he puts into the family. By focusing on the little things, you will reinforce the positive energy and that will lead to bigger things."**

Maria stays relaxed and begins to remember things her husband has done to help out with the children. She then remembers several times when he helped out with dinner, or with cleaning up afterward. She remembers how he has played with the children on weekends and given her time to do the meditation after work. She then remembers how often he does smile at her and how often he is affectionate. The exercise seems to flow easily, and she is surprised how easy it is to center on the positive feelings and remember the good times.

When the session ends, Maria reflects on the experience. She realizes that she and her husband have a lot of love and caring in their relationship. She also notes that she often complains, not because her husband hasn't helped but because he hasn't helped exactly the way she wanted him to. Maria decides that demanding he do things just the way she wants is a little unfair and that she could show him more appreciation for the tasks he completes.

INSTRUCTIONS FOR RELATIONSHIP APPLICATION 1: BUILDING POSITIVE ENERGY

- Remember your intention to center on the positive aspects of the relationship.
- If you are feeling tense, do a calming exercise for a couple of minutes.
- Then remember any actions the other person did that were kind and loving. Center on the positive aspects of the relationship by returning your awareness to these types of memories.
- If negative thoughts or memories come up, identify them and disengage from them by remembering the positive ones.
- If you get caught by the negative memories, disengage by identifying the emotions associated with them and then center on something physical, such as the sensations in your lower abdomen or the sensations of air moving in and out of your nose.
- When you feel calm, go back to centering on the positive aspects of the relationship.
- At the end of the session, reflect on your experience, especially noting any positive things you hadn't remembered before. Also note any patterns in the distracting thoughts or sensations.

BRIAN'S AND MARIA'S RESULTS FROM BUILDING POSITIVE ENERGY PRACTICE

After one week of practicing Building Positive Energy, Brian is able to do it more easily. The negative thoughts that were upsetting him are much weaker. He has reflected that much of his irritation about how his son dresses and keeps his room are things that Brian irritated his parents with when he was a child. He still wants his son to improve, but he realizes that improvement will be more likely if he reinforces the positive behaviors instead of criticizing the negative ones.

Maria has practiced Building Positive Energy for a week. She feels her emotions toward her husband becoming steadier, more consistently warm. She finds it easier to show appreciation for the positive things he does. This is making the atmosphere around the house much warmer. He is also becoming more receptive to her when she does complain.

RELATIONSHIP APPLICATION 2: CLOSENESS DURING CONFLICT

Conflict will arise eventually in every one of your relationships. If you want to have successful relationships, you will have to be able to resolve conflicts. In our experience, most people avoid conflict because it makes them uncomfortable. If the problem were to be discussed, strong negative emotions might be triggered, so the issue is usually avoided. Of course this doesn't resolve the problem. The hot issue is not discussed and this lack of discussion leads to increased coldness.

Fortunately, the meditation techniques you have learned can be used to make it easier for you to resolve conflicts. As we discussed in the chapter on performance, your mind doesn't know the difference between a vividly imagined event and a real event. You can use meditation to reduce the influence of your negative emotions while you are in the conflict. You can identify buttons before they are pushed, and desensitize yourself to them. After you have practiced doing this in meditation, it is much safer to address the issue with the other person.

This exercise has an added benefit. Often the problem issue is associated with other fears or irritations you have about the relationship that are hidden from you. This practice can make you aware of those hidden issues, helping you to get clear about what really needs to be dealt with before you talk with the other person.

You will get better results with this exercise if you have practiced Building Positive Energy for a couple of weeks before starting this one. In that way you have been experiencing the love and caring there is in the relationship before you start to work on issues.

BRIAN'S FIRST EXPERIENCE WITH CLOSENESS DURING CONFLICT

Brian and his wife have regular arguments about money. He gets upset about the amount she spends, but whenever they try to talk about it, they have an argument or even a verbal fight. He becomes loud and accusatory, while she gets hurt and sullen. This causes a bad feeling between them that can last for days. The subject of money has become so hot that Brian usually does not even bring it up. He just tries to put it out of his mind.

Brian plans to use Closeness During Conflict to help him talk reasonably about some of the financial issues without getting so upset that it leads to a fight. Knowing that this is an emotional subject, he figures he will have to spend several sessions on it.

After Brian focuses on his intention to be able to talk calmly about finances, he remembers an important point from his teacher: **"Make sure you center on something calming at the beginning of the exercise. Then if you experience intense emotions, you can use that center to calm yourself."** As Brian sits quietly, he centers on the thoughts "Calm" as he inhales and "Relaxed" as he exhales. Once he is relaxed, he thinks about the last credit card bill he saw. Remembering that it was higher than expected, he feels a tightness in his stomach and a tension in his jaw and throat. He identifies these sensations, disengages from them, and concentrates again on the memory of the credit card bill.

Brian then identifies a number of familiar thoughts. "She's always spending money." "Why does she have to buy everything she sees?" Brian identifies these thoughts, but can't disengage from them and go back to remembering the bill. He is too upset. **"When you are unable to disengage from negative thoughts, identify the emotion behind those thoughts and center on something calming until you feel peaceful."** Brian identifies the emotion that is associated with his thoughts as anger and disengages from them by centering on the thoughts "Calm – Relaxed." After a minute or so, Brian feels calmer and is able to remember the credit card bill again.

Brian has to repeat this several times, but each time it is easier to disengage from his anger. Then as he is remembering the credit card bill, he notices that he is thinking about what his wife has bought for his children. He identifies this thought, and then notices that he feels somewhat pleased. This emotion surprises him, and he identifies it and goes back to remembering the bill.

Suddenly Brian feels like a door has opened up in his mind, and a large number of memories, thoughts, and emotions pours through. He remembers being a child and wanting clothes that his family was too poor to buy. He thinks about the things he wishes he could buy his children. He thinks about the vacations he would like to take his wife on, but that they can't afford. He wonders if he is really providing enough for his family. He wonders if his wife is really satisfied with him. He feels despondent and inadequate.

Brian is shocked by the intensity of his experience. He feels almost drowned by the flood of emotion that has poured in. He hears the voice of his teacher faintly, **"This exercise can bring up strong emotions. If you are feeling overwhelmed, remember your anchor. Center on what calms you until you can disengage from the emotions."** Brian focuses his awareness on the sensations in his abdomen and thinks "Calm" as he inhales and "Relaxed" as he exhales. His months of practice have made this a powerful calming anchor for him. He feels the emotions of sadness and inadequacy fade, and feels his body relax.

Brian feels exhausted, and realizes he has to stop the exercise. As he reflects on the experience, he realizes that the issue is not really how much his wife is spending. It's more about his fears that she does not think he is a good provider. He also reflects that he will need to repeat this exercise several more times before he will be able to talk coherently with his wife about this issue.

MARIA'S FIRST EXPERIENCE WITH CLOSENESS DURING CONFLICT

Maria has the impression that she is fighting with her children almost constantly about the messes they make. It seems that she is scolding them every day. She knows that she is overreacting to what is rather normal behavior for young children, but she can't seem to stop herself. She wants to change this pattern.

As Maria starts her first session of Closeness During Conflict, she remembers, **"After remembering your intention, center on something calming that can serve as an anchor if you are experiencing intense feelings."** Maria thinks about her desire to respond more constructively to the messes her children make. She then centers on the phrase "My face is soft and gentle." She has been using that as a brief relaxation technique for several weeks, and it has a strong calming effect on her.

After a few seconds Maria feels relaxed, and she concentrates on the last time she found her children's books and toys scattered all over the living room after she had told them to clean up. Immediately, her body tenses, and she feels angry. She identifies the tension and anger and disengages from them, going back to the memory of the messy room. The anger returns, and she has the additional thought that her children are ignoring her. This thought intensifies her anger. Maria identifies the thought and the anger and tries to disengage from them, but cannot. She focuses on the phrase "My face is soft and gentle," but notices that her face feels hard and angry. **"If focusing on something calming does not work, then focus on a positive aspect of the relationship with the person you are having difficulty with."** Maria remembers and concentrates on some of the cute things her children have done. She feels her anger subside.

Going back to concentrating on the memory of the messy room, she now feels frustration. The thought associated with the frustration is that she has told her children a thousand times to clean up, but with no results. Maria identifies the frustration and associated thought and disengages from them by refocusing on the positive memories of her children.

She repeats this process of switching between the memory of the messy room, identifying the thoughts and emotions that are evoked, and disengaging from them by remembering positive scenes with her children.

After several repetitions, Maria realizes she is feeling fear. As she identifies this emotion, she realizes that she is thinking that her children have no discipline. She is afraid that they will grow up to be irresponsible, that they will be delinquents or derelicts. Maria is shocked by these fearful thoughts. She identifies them and disengages from them, focusing on the positive memories. Maria then realizes how silly these fears are. Her children are well behaved most of the time. She feels a sense of relief and realizes that now her face is soft and gentle.

Maria refocuses on the memory of the messy room and soon has the insight that her children might feel overwhelmed by her demand that they clean it unassisted. As she realizes this, her alarm beeps, signaling the end of the session. Maria finishes the exercise by reflecting on her new insights. She observes how she needs to get rid of the illogical fears that are fueling much of her anger and frustration. She also reflects on how she will have to try a different approach to getting her children to clean up their messes.

INSTRUCTIONS FOR RELATIONSHIP APPLICATION 2: CLOSENESS DURING CONFLICT

- Sit or lie down in a comfortable position in which you can completely relax.
- Remember your intention: to be able to handle a difficult interpersonal issue while staying calm and maintaining a sense of respect and connection.
- Center on a calming sensation or image. This will be your anchor throughout the exercise.
- Once you are calm, concentrate on the issue you are in conflict about. You can often do this by concentrating on the memory of an event where the other person did something to upset you (or neglected to do something). Focus on what the other person did or said.
- Attend to the thoughts, sensations, and emotions that come up by identifying and disengaging from them. If you start to feel agitated or overwhelmed, go back to centering on the

calming sensation or image. If that doesn't work, focus on a positive memory about the person.

- IMPORTANT: As you identify thoughts, sensations, and emotions, pay particular attention to those that seem new to you, or those that seem deeper than the usual thoughts you have about the issue.
- Continue to stay calm while you imagine the conflict and attend to the thoughts, and so on, that arise.
- As you end your concentration, reflect on any ideas that come to mind. Be especially aware of any ideas that seem to give you a different perspective on the conflict.
- Practice this until you can remain calm throughout the exercise and have a sense that you can really experience the other person's perspective as well as your own.

BRIAN'S AND MARIA'S RESULTS FROM CLOSENESS DURING CONFLICT PRACTICE

Brian had to practice Closeness During Conflict several times before he could stay calm during the exercise. He realized that the financial issues would not be dealt with overnight, but he knew that he could stay calmer during a discussion. He also recognized that his sadness at not having all the money he wanted to buy things for his family was what triggered his angry reaction.

Brian talked with his wife about some guidelines for discussing finances together. He told her he got tense because he wished he made more money than he does, but that that was not her fault. He said that if he got tense during a discussion from now on, then he would ask for a time-out for a few minutes so he could calm himself. He also requested that she try to avoid being critical of how much money he made, as that would fuel his sadness and frustration. His wife agreed to work with those rules. She also reassured him that she was quite satisfied with his income, and that she was grateful that he was working on improving their relationship. Their next discussion about bills was difficult and he had to take several time-outs, but it was also more constructive, and there was no anger or bitterness afterward.

Maria practiced Closeness During Conflict one more time, concentrating on the messes her children make. It was much easier to stay calm in the second session, and she realized that if her children were really feeling overwhelmed by her demands that they clean up, then she needed to act differently. She decided to change her approach by helping them get started. This required her to participate for most of the cleaning up the first couple of times, but it still took less time and energy on her part than when she used to get upset. After those first few times, she noticed that her children were beginning to require less participation on her part and were doing more of the work themselves. They still seemed to want her to be present for most of it, but she was able to relax during the process and even find it enjoyable. Once, after cleaning up their rooms with her, the children even followed her around the house helping her with the rest of the cleaning. Their help did not speed things up greatly, but it was fun and it put to rest Maria's fears that her children were irresponsible.

RELATIONSHIP APPLICATION 3:
SPACE WITHOUT DISTANCE

Many times we feel crowded in a relationship. As much as we love the people around us, we feel as if they are too close. We want space. That need for space is important and often healthy. It is a sign that we want to grow, to explore other aspects of ourselves. The problem comes because most people equate space with distance. When they want space, they feel they need to become more distant from the people around them. Sometimes this causes a person to create conflict in order to make others back off and satisfy the person's need for space.

However, the space that we want in a relationship is psychological space. For the mind, space and distance do not have to be the same. Remember, spaciousness is a natural mental quality. Your mind has all the space it needs. When you know how to experience that space, you do not need to become more distant from the ones you love.

Imagine that you and the other people in your life were living on a flat surface, with no idea of the space above or below you. Then it would be natural to feel crowded when they got close to you. Now imagine that you suddenly realized that there was lots of room above you and below you. Suddenly you would experience plenty of space, without having to move away from anyone. In fact, you could even get closer to the others and still feel you had plenty of space.

Practicing Space Without Distance does this for you. You are able to experience having space to grow and change without having to distance yourself from those you love. Doing so uses your mind's natural quality of spaciousness and allows you to be creative so that you are able to both meet your needs for space and maintain closeness.

BRIAN'S FIRST EXPERIENCE WITH SPACE WITHOUT DISTANCE

Brian is able to talk about money and other issues more easily with his wife now. This has eased the tension in their relationship. However, one continuing source of difficulty arises when Brian is feeling stressed and wants to be alone. When this happens, his wife seems to sense that something is wrong, and asks him questions. This increases his stress, because he knows that his desire to withdraw and be alone is upsetting his wife. He becomes even more quiet and distant. In response, his wife often gets visibly upset and accuses him of not communicating. When he hears that, Brian gets so upset that he often has to leave the house for a while.

Brian is interested in Space Without Distance. He feels that if he can learn to feel space without making his wife feel distance, they will each feel more comfortable. Brian sits down to practice and begins by focusing his intention in order to feel the space he needs while staying emotionally close to his wife. He goes quickly through the Autonomic Relaxation exercise so that he can relax deeply.

Brian thinks about the warmth and love he and his wife feel for each other. He quickly feels the positive emotions he has toward her. He then does the opening technique of imagining he is on a mountaintop. He experiences the vastness and feels as if there is an immense space around him. Within a couple of minutes, Brian feels like he is high above things. The air is clear and crisp, and it is very quiet. He watches the things he is stressed about get more distant. He then recalls the warm feelings he has for his wife. He imagines that she is sitting near him on the mountaintop, not crowding him, just being present. He can still feel the space above, around, and below him.

As Brian does this, he sees images related to the things that stress him: his job, the economy, worries about his kids. He focuses more strongly on the sense of vastness and allows those images to move farther away. At the same time, he thinks again about the positive feelings he has for his wife. Her image stays close and the stressful images move off into the distance.

Brian is enjoying this. He is experiencing the warmth, love, and presence of his partner while separating from the stresses that cause him to shut down. He realizes that he can feel comfortable with her presence if she is willing to sit more quietly and ask fewer questions. He reflects on this new insight and realizes he has never tried just sitting quietly and lovingly with his wife. He decides this will be worth attempting. He then reorients to the time and place, flexes his arms and legs, and opens his eyes.

MARIA'S FIRST EXPERIENCE WITH SPACE WITHOUT DISTANCE

Maria has been pleased with the results of Closeness During Conflict. She is handling her children's messes without yelling or nagging. Nonetheless, there are times when she still feels irritated by the disorder around the house. This does not just occur because of her children's messes. Her husband will also leave his clothes lying around or throw his jacket over a chair when he comes home from work. These events sometimes make Maria wish that she lived by herself, when everything would stay in its proper place. It is then that she feels annoyed and acts irritably.

Maria decides to use Space Without Distance to reduce her sensitivity to some of the normal disorder in the household. She starts by remembering her intention to be at ease and feel that she has her own space in spite of the presence of the other people at home. Maria relaxes and then remembers some of the things she enjoys about her family members. She concentrates on the positive feelings generated by those memories. She experiences the love and caring she has for her husband and children.

Maria then uses the opening technique she has had success with before. She focuses on the experience of her body expanding as she inhales and contracting as she exhales. Soon she feels the familiar sense of drifting. She continues to bring the positive memories of her family to mind while she drifts comfortably. She begins to see many other scenes from family life flowing from one into another. She recognizes that she is still herself even though her husband and children influence her. As she enjoys the floating sensations, she experiences a whole new dimension of her being that is free and unhindered by the needs and actions of her family members. Her mind relaxes even more, and even the images fade into a comfortable sense of peacefulness.

Maria enjoys the experience, and when her alarm beeps, she reflects on how she needs to separate who she is from what she does. She picks up after her children and occasionally her husband, but that is not who she is. She is a not a maid, even if she has to clean up at times.

INSTRUCTIONS FOR RELATIONSHIP APPLICATION 3: SPACE WITHOUT DISTANCE

- Start by sitting or lying in a comfortable position.
- Remember your intention to experience a sense of personal space while staying close to the other person.
- Center on a positive memory of the other person. Attend to thoughts, emotions, and sensations that arise.
- Concentrate on the positive feeling you have for the other person.

- Use an opening technique to experience a sense of vastness while staying connected to the positive feeling you have for the other person. For example, imagine being on a mountaintop and seeing the image of the other person at a comfortable distance.
- Continue to remind yourself of the positive feelings as well as the vastness until you experience a sense of space as well as the positive feelings.
- While experiencing the sense of space, attend to thoughts, images, and ideas that come to mind.
- As you come out of the meditation, reflect on the ideas and images that came up, and take notes on any that seem relevant or surprising.
- This exercise helps bring our creativity into the relationship, helping us to resolve our need for growth as an individual while still maintaining emotional closeness.

BRIAN'S AND MARIA'S RESULTS FROM SPACE WITHOUT DISTANCE PRACTICE

Several days after doing the session of Space Without Distance, Brian comes home stressed out. He feels the familiar desire to be silent and withdraw. His wife seems to sense that and asks the usual question, "What's wrong?" Just as Brian starts to answer "Nothing," he catches himself. Instead, he asks, "Do you have a few minutes?" His wife seems surprised by the question but answers, "Yes." Luckily the house is quiet, so they sit down on the couch together. Brian says, "I'm OK, I don't need to talk. But I do want to sit close to you for a few minutes." He puts his arm around her, and she leans up against him.

Brian closes his eyes and remembers the experience from the

session of Space Without Distance. He can feel the pleasant warmth of his wife's body against his. He imagines being on the mountain-top with all the pressures and worries of the day falling off into the distance. He connects more strongly with the presence of his wife. He can feel the freedom of the space and the comfortable warmth of her next to him. He feels his whole body relax, and he feels his wife relax also. They sit together for a few more minutes and then Brian says, "You know, I love you and I'm really glad you're here." His wife responds with a warm hug and they get up together.

Brian realizes that he doesn't feel as withdrawn now. While he still wants some time by himself, he feels comfortably connected to his wife. His wife also seems to be more comfortable. She is not pursuing him with questions, and the evening passes peacefully.

ONE EVENING, after Maria has practiced Space Without Distance a couple of times, her husband comes home and leaves his coat draped over the living room chair. Maria is ready to make a sharp remark when she remembers her experiences from the Space Without Distance exercise. Feeling a need for space at the moment, she takes a deep breath and imagines space filling her whole body. Then she exhales and imagines plenty of space around her, especially between her and the coat on the chair.

Maria feels her mind clear and then notices that her husband looks a little upset. She asks him if he wants some quiet time or if he wants to go for a little walk. He looks a little surprised, and agrees that a short walk would be nice. He picks up his jacket, puts it on, and heads out the door. A short time later, her husband returns. His mood is lighter, and when he takes off his jacket, he hangs it up in the closet. Maria smiles to herself. She has used a lot less energy and achieved better results than if she had reacted in her usual manner.

REVIEW OF RELATIONSHIP APPLICATIONS

Having peaceful relationships, with a partner, family members, and others helps you to maintain a sense of inner peace. You need more than an absence of fighting to have peaceful relationships. You must experience the relationship as being positive and caring. You must be able to resolve difficult issues instead of avoid them. Finally, you must be able to grow personally while staying connected to the other person.

These three applications of meditation counter common tendencies that disrupt the positive interactions in a relationship. By practicing them, you will be able to improve your relationship with your partner, if you have one. You will also be able to improve your relationships with your children, friends, and colleagues at work.

Like the applications in the previous chapters, these three applications are best practiced in sequence. Building Positive Energy will create a more positive atmosphere in the relationship. It is an antidote to taking positive things for granted. Building Positive Energy generates results quickly. You will often experience a change in your feelings about the relationship after only one or two sessions.

Closeness During Conflict is an important exercise because it enables you to practice working through a hot issue before you actually talk about it. It enables you to break the common pattern of avoiding discussions about difficult topics. Because Closeness During Conflict can bring up a lot of negative feelings, it is helpful to have practiced Building Positive Energy successfully first. That will keep you from being overwhelmed by negative emotions when you do the exercise.

The third application, Space Without Distance, helps resolve the paradox of needing a sense of freedom and space while also remaining emotionally close to another person. It brings creativity into the relationship and allows you to come up with new responses to old situations. You will get better results using Space Without Distance if you get familiar with the previous two exercises first.

If you want to focus on improving a relationship over an extended period of time, then after you have had experience with all three applications, we recommend you practice Building Positive Energy for a couple of minutes at least once per day. You should use Closeness During Conflict to help you talk through specific issues. If you are enjoying a time when there do not seem to be any specific difficulties in the relationship, then you may not need to practice this application. Use Space Without Distance when you are feeling a need for personal space or personal growth. Again, there may be times when you do not need this technique.

10 spirituality: increasing the experience of love in your life

SPIRITUALITY refers to the quality of our relationship to transcendence and love. The amount of peace in your life is directly related to your ability to connect with love. Your health, your performance, and even your relationships are all somewhat out of your control. The aspect of your life that you have the most influence over is your experience of love.

Every now and then, we have experiences of transcendence and love that break into the daily routine. Those experiences are usually rare and fleeting. Then ordinary reality returns. However, we can cultivate our spirituality so that we will experience that transcendent love on a daily, even constant basis. Meditation was developed by spiritual traditions in order to make the experience of transcendence and love accessible and more a part of everyday experience.

We are using the word *love* to indicate the presence or the idea of what people may call "God" or "Jesus" or "Universal

Consciousness" or any number of other words—in other words, unconditional love and compassion that is beyond any conceptual definition. Any true experience of it defies description. Feel free to substitute your own word in its place, as long as the ideas of love and transcendence are present.

Meditation is a practical and rapid way to increase the experience of love in your life. Many people have difficulty believing that spiritual techniques can be so ordinary. People make them harder than they really are. But the techniques we describe are simple and effective. They are within your capabilities and are not meant for a spiritual elite. All that you need is familiarity with the basic techniques described in part 1, and the willingness to be persistent in practice.

We will describe three techniques for increasing the experience of love in your life. We begin with a simple technique and move to more complex ones. The most important result of practice is that you will experience love, not just while you are meditating but more and more spontaneously throughout the day.

SPIRITUALITY APPLICATION 1: CENTERING PRAYER

One way to experience love in meditation is to stop and sit quietly. The presence of love is always here. So instead of being noisy with your mind and chattering away at the presence of love, or running around trying to find it somewhere, you simply place yourself in a receptive state of mind, and listen. This process is called Centering Prayer. It is not passive because you have to use some energy to keep yourself quiet and receptive. But it is also not active or seeking. You exert mental energy to stay in the receptive and quiet attitude and then wait and listen.

This method of prayer uses centering and attending skills. In order to move into a state that is receptive to the presence of love, you center on the idea of love. You then use attending skills to listen and to disengage from anything that tries to distract you. The result is an experience of inner quiet and connection with a loving presence. Mental noise gets fainter and doesn't matter as much. You feel as if you are where you have been trying to get all along.

Centering on the idea of love requires some skill and practice. The idea of love is more abstract than physical sensations, images of health or performance, and feelings toward another person. The applications in the earlier chapters will have helped your mind become more comfortable centering on abstract ideas.

To center on the idea of love, spend some time thinking about what transcendent love means to you. Think about love and how it is expressed in your life and in the world. Think about the things associated with love: caring, peace, joy, and humor. You might find yourself thinking that love can exist as a being, God maybe, or you might simply find yourself thinking of qualities associated with love. After thinking about love for a little while, choose one term that seems to best represent the idea of love to you. Words such as Love, Peace, Joy, God, Jesus, Buddha, Hope, Wonder, Divine Mother, Father, Consciousness, and One are commonly used.

It is important that you think about transcendent love before choosing the term. That is what gives it meaning for you. The term becomes your "sacred word."

Once you have chosen your sacred word, then you can use it as an anchor to help you center on the presence of love—that is, to practice Centering Prayer. During the prayer time you use the term you have chosen in order to help you disengage from any thoughts or sensations that distract you from the presence of love. Even thoughts about love can be distractions, so when your mind gets noisy, identify the noise and then mentally repeat the word to help you disengage from the distraction.

BRIAN'S FIRST EXPERIENCE WITH CENTERING PRAYER

Brian has thought about transcendent love for a few days. The term that has kept coming to his mind has been *peace*. He has decided to use that as his sacred word.

As he sits down for his morning meditation session, he remembers his intention. He intends to sit quietly and be receptive to love and peace. He then spends a couple of minutes centering on his breath until he feels relaxed. Then he thinks the word "Peace" and lets his mind reflect on the idea of peace and love. He notices a lot of thoughts about love and peace. Then he finds he is thinking about some of the negative things that go on in the world as well. He identifies these thoughts as negative distractions and disengages from them by thinking "Peace" several times. The negative thoughts subside and he feels a sense of quiet followed almost immediately by thoughts about love. The thoughts seem attractive and he starts to explore them. **"Even thoughts about love can become distracting. If they arise, just identify them and disengage from them by thinking of your sacred word."** Brian does that, and the sense of quiet returns. Various other thoughts arise, and he disengages from them easily. However, his mind seems to want to keep thinking actively about love and peace. **"Staying quiet and receptive is difficult for people who analyze and think a lot. Being receptive is an activity they are not used to. By disengaging from the thoughts about love, you will experience a deeper connection with love. The thoughts will return after the session. You are not banishing them forever, so sometimes telling them 'Later' is helpful."**

Brian thanks his mind for thinking such positive thoughts, but then tells it "Later" and repeats his sacred word "Peace" gently to himself several times. Again the sense of quiet returns and he feels as if something has joined him. He continues to sit quietly enjoying the experience of peace until the session ends.

He then reflects on his experience and notes how Centering Prayer and thinking about love are quite different. He realizes that he will have to practice disengaging from his tendency to analyze. He also notes that he is now having several thoughts about peace and love that are new to him.

MARIA'S FIRST EXPERIENCE WITH CENTERING PRAYER

Maria is excited about using meditation for spirituality. She first spends some time thinking about her sacred word. This is surprisingly difficult for her. She felt sure that she would use "God" as her sacred word, but when she starts thinking about God as love, she realizes that God is just a word for her and not very connected to a deep experience of love. After spending some days reflecting on love and her understanding of God's love for her, she feels more of a connection between the word "God" and the deep love behind it. "God" is now, truly, her sacred word.

Maria begins her session of Centering Prayer by focusing on her intention. Her intention for this session is to sit quietly in the presence of a loving God. She gently repeats the word "God" to herself with every exhalation, and becomes more and more relaxed. After a few minutes her body settles and her mind becomes quieter.

She has a series of thoughts about work and her family, but she is able to identify these and disengage from them easily. When she catches herself thinking about something, she identifies the thoughts and disengages from them by thinking "God" to herself. Soon she feels quite peaceful, as if she is sitting comfortably with a loving friend. Suddenly she thinks, "Is this all there is to it? Maybe I should be doing something else?" She starts to worry, but remembers,

"When you are centered on the presence of love, everything gets quiet and there is nothing more to do. Simply stay in that presence, and if something distracts you, disengage from it, then mentally say your sacred word once or twice until you re-center on the presence of love."

Maria feels reassured, and is able to disengage from the worry and go back to enjoying the experience. Then she starts to worry again. She remembers some things she's done that weren't so nice, such as snapping at her husband and children. The thought comes "You don't deserve this, you aren't good enough for it." **"When you start to enjoy Centering Prayer, you might feel you don't deserve the experience. But it is not a question of deserving. You simply accept the enjoyment as a gift and realize that practicing Centering Prayer will help you become a better person. So identify those thoughts as accusations and disengage from them using your sacred word. You are loved with your imperfections. If you have difficulty disengaging, simply assert 'I'm sorry' mentally in order to help you disengage."**

Maria acknowledges the thoughts and identifies them as accusations. She thinks, "I apologize," and then repeats "God" several times to herself until she is disengaged from her doubting thoughts. The rest of her meditation session consists of periods of quiet loving presence and occasional distracting thoughts. It feels quite restful. When her session ends and she reflects on the experience, she realizes her mind has become much quieter than usual. She feels a sense of inner peace and satisfaction, as if everything has been taken care of and there is no need for her to do anything.

INSTRUCTIONS FOR SPIRITUALITY APPLICATION 1: CENTERING PRAYER

- This is a basic form of contemplative prayer used in a number of spiritual traditions. The idea is to let the mind center on the idea of love. The mind is centering on an idea, not on an image or words.
- Pick a word that symbolizes the concept or presence of love to you. This word will help you re-center on the presence of love. The word must be meaningful to you, as it will become your "sacred word." Use the same word from session to session. Your sacred word will you bring your awareness back to the idea of love.
- Remember your intention to center your mind on the idea of love.
- Mentally repeat your sacred word several times to yourself. Allow your mind to center on the idea symbolized by the word. Once your mind is connected with the idea, let go of repeating the word.
- As long as your mind is quiet, just rest. If you get distracted, then repeat your sacred word to yourself until your mind quiets again.
- *Reflection:* After the event, recall your experience and note any patterns in the distracting thoughts or sensations.

BRIAN'S AND MARIA'S RESULTS FROM CENTERING PRAYER PRACTICE

Brian has been practicing Centering Prayer for one month. He does it three times per week, and alternates the basic techniques of attending, concentrating, and opening in his other three weekly practice sessions. Brian finds Centering Prayer enjoyable. He is able to feel quiet and peaceful within a few minutes. Then he just rests there. As a result, he has begun to feel like he is a naturally peaceful person. He had considered himself rather tough and aggressive, but now senses that the toughness is only an exterior; he is really quite peaceful underneath. He can use the toughness if he has to, but it is hardly all that he is. This allows him to express his natural peace more easily.

Maria has alternated Centering Prayer with the basic attending, concentrating, and opening techniques for the last month. During Centering Prayer she experiences a deep quiet. This experience of deep quiet has helped her feel less urgency during the day. She has a sense that things will work out and that she does not need to be chronically hurried.

While Maria enjoys Centering Prayer, she also feels a little bored. She wants to do more than just be quiet with God. When she queried her teacher about this, he responded, **"Some people find Centering Prayer too quiet. It is an effective form of prayer, but you can move on to the next practice, which requires more mental activity."**

SPIRITUALITY APPLICATION 2:
PRACTICING THE PRESENCE OF LOVE

Centering Prayer is a good foundation for using meditation in prayer. Still, many people, such as Maria, want to be more mentally active during prayer. They also want something they can use throughout the day.

Practicing the Presence of Love meets these needs. While Centering Prayer gives the experience of love during quiet and stillness, Practicing the Presence of Love makes the experience of love available when we're active. It also strengthens our connection with love so that the experience is available even during noisy or chaotic situations.

To start this technique, concentrate on the idea that love is within you and surrounding you. While you concentrate on that idea, you are also to attend to thoughts, images, sensations, and emotions that arise. Disengage from things that distract you from the idea of love and concentrate on the thoughts, images, and emotions that are related to it. As you do this, you will create an increasingly vivid experience of love within and around you. You then maintain that experience by continuing to concentrate on it for as long as is comfortable.

Practicing the Presence of Love is done using both extended and brief sessions. The extended sessions build a strong, tangible connection with love using a combination of attending and concentrating skills. The brief sessions enable you to restore that connection instantly, no matter where you are, and no matter what is happening around you.

BRIAN'S FIRST EXPERIENCE WITH PRACTICING THE PRESENCE OF LOVE

Brian starts his session of Practicing the Presence of Love by focusing his intention to experience peace as a presence both inside and outside himself. He concentrates on the idea of peace being inside him as well as outside him. His mind is somewhat noisy, so he identifies the random thoughts, sensations, and emotions that appear. He is able to disengage from these just by concentrating on the idea of peace inside and around him. After a short time, his mind gets quiet and he does indeed feel peaceful inside himself.

But Brian is still not aware of a sense of peace outside of him; it all seems to be within. As he concentrates on the idea of peace surrounding him, an image starts to appear in his mind. As he attends to it, he notices that it is a figure of a monk wearing a hooded robe. He cannot see the monk's face, just the outline of the hooded robe. An aura of peace seems to flow from the monk and surround him. He then feels this peace flow around him, resonating with the peace he already experienced inside. Brian is startled and wonders if he should disengage from this image. **"If an image or thought comes to mind that increases your experience of peace, then just be aware of it. You do not need to disengage from it. Experience its presence and the increased peace it brings. If it fades out on its own, let it go, but you do not need to disengage from it."**

Brian observes the image and experiences the sense of peace filling and surrounding him. The image fades after a few minutes and he returns to identifying and disengaging from random mental noise. As he reflects on the experience at the end of the session, he has a vivid memory of the monk's image, and feels the peaceful aura of that figure. He remembers what his teacher said: **"Pick a mental or physical cue that connects you with the experience and that you can use frequently during the day."** Brian decides that the image of the monk can be a mental cue to remind him of the experience of peace.

MARIA'S FIRST EXPERIENCE WITH PRACTICING THE PRESENCE OF LOVE

Maria has wanted to become more active in applying meditation to spirituality. She is hoping that Practicing the Presence of Love will satisfy her desire. Maria sits down for her meditation session and remembers her intention to feel the presence of God within and around her. Maria then does her usual relaxation technique of centering on the phrase "My face is soft and gentle" for a couple of minutes. That gets her into a calm and comfortable state. She then concentrates on the idea of God being around and within her.

Maria has the intellectual understanding that God is everywhere, but when she concentrates on the idea, she realizes that she has little emotional experience of it. **"We often find that we have little real experience of the presence of love. Simply concentrate on the idea of love and wait expectantly for images, thoughts, or feelings to arise. This is similar to what you do in the basic concentration technique. Attend to images, thoughts, or feelings that come up, and disengage from those that are not helpful. Focus on those that are helpful."**

Maria waits expectantly, concentrating on the idea of God being around and inside her. After a number of random thoughts that she disengages from, the ideas of patience and understanding arise. It is as if there is a presence around her that understands her intimately and has infinite patience with her. As she attends to this presence, she has the sense that it is feminine, like a mother who is cradling her. At first Maria wants to reject the experience of God being feminine. Her Christian teachers never talked about God in feminine terms, but she remembers a comment from her meditation teacher: **"People are often surprised to learn that Judaism and Christianity describe God in feminine as well as masculine terms. For example, the prophet Isaiah uses the metaphor of God as nursing Israel, hardly a masculine activity. If your experience isn't consistent with how you've conceived of God in the past, that's OK."**

Maria relaxes and concentrates on the feeling of being cradled by this understanding and patient presence. As she rests in the experience, she senses her own patience and understanding. While she has often criticized herself for not being patient, she is now realizing that she is actually a patient and understanding person. Maria enjoys this feeling. She also feels safe and loved in the arms of a "motherly" presence.

As she rests there, Maria remembers times when she was patient, and others when she was not so patient. She senses that the presence surrounding her understands that she tries, and that it is patient with her. Maria realizes she needs to be more patient with herself as well as with others.

As she finishes the exercise by reflecting on the experience, Maria decides that the cue for recalling this presence of patience and understanding will be to take a deep breath and think "Patience" to herself.

INSTRUCTIONS FOR SPIRITUALITY APPLICATION 2: PRACTICING THE PRESENCE OF LOVE

- This application uses both an extended meditation and a brief practice.
- Remember your intention to experience the presence of love within you and around you.
- Concentrate on the idea that love is within you right now as well as surrounding you.
- Attend to your experience as you concentrate. Notice your thoughts, posture, emotional state, and attendant sensations. Think about how you would speak, move, look at things, and present yourself if love were with you and within you.
- As your experience becomes more vivid, set a mental or physical cue for this state.
- Continue to experience this as long as is comfortable.
- Reflect on the experience and how it differs from the way you usually experience life.
- Several times throughout the day, use the cue and reexperience the sense of love within and around you.

TIPS FOR THE EXTENDED PRACTICE OF PRACTICING THE PRESENCE OF LOVE

- Imagine that someone or something representing love is really there with you.
- As you get a sense of this presence next to you, start to feel the presence of love within you as well.
- Imagine you are seeing with the eyes of love, speaking with the voice of love, and touching with the hands of love.
- This practice can take a good deal of energy. If you get tired, go back to Centering Prayer.
- During the reflection phase, allow your mind to create a cue that will reconnect you with the presence of love. This cue may be a physical sign, a mental image, or a mental word.

TIPS FOR THE BRIEF PRACTICE OF PRACTICING THE PRESENCE OF LOVE

- Our most important tip is that you practice, the more frequently the better.
- Don't judge the results. Just accept them. Sometimes when you remember the cue, you will feel a strong presence. Sometimes you will feel a weak presence, or nothing at all. As you practice more, the experiences will become more perceptible.

BRIAN'S AND MARIA'S RESULTS FROM PRACTICING THE PRESENCE OF LOVE

Brian has worked on Practicing the Presence of Love for a couple of weeks. The first few days, he forgot to do the brief version except for a couple of times at the end of the day. He was able to experience the presence of peace when he did the extended version. After a couple of days of forgetting to do the brief version, Brian set his watch so that it would beep every hour. He promised himself that every day for the next week he would do the brief exercise every time his watch beeped, or as soon as possible afterward.

After that week, Brian now feels as if the peaceful presence has taken on a life of its own. Sometimes he feels peaceful spontaneously. He is not turning on the news as often during his drive home from work. Once, while driving, someone had suddenly cut in front of him. Brian got angry and began to glare at the other driver. Suddenly, he had the strong impression that his monk friend was sitting in the passenger seat looking at him. Brian felt embarrassed at his angry reaction. He reflected that the other driver probably wasn't trying to offend him personally. It seemed like his monk friend was smiling peacefully at him, and he laughed as his anger and the tension drained away.

Maria started with a lot of resolve to do the brief practice frequently. However, she forgot to do it completely the first day after doing the extended session, and she did not remember on the second day until the evening. She was frustrated, but remembered her teacher saying, **"The brief version of Practicing the Presence of Love is hard to remember when you first start. Remember to have patience with yourself. If you continue to practice the extended version and set up specific times to do the brief version, it will become a habit."**

Maria decided she would practice before and after meals, and before and after driving. That gave her at least eight brief practice sessions per day, without interrupting any activities. Maria was able to notice a difference after one week: Her days feel smoother. She is more patient with herself and those around her.

One Saturday evening, she began to get upset with her children after telling them for what seemed like the thousandth time to pick up their toys. All the progress she had made earlier to be more accepting of their messes seemed to disappear. She was just as frustrated as ever, and about ready to start yelling. Suddenly, she felt the now-familiar presence of a patient, understanding mother cradling her. She realized that God was very patient with her. God had asked her far more than a thousand times to stop speaking angrily, and still was patient with her. Maria took a deep breath and said "Patience" to herself. She felt the understanding, patient presence of God flow into her. Instead of saying the angry words that had been on her lips, she said, "Mommy needs some help or she is going to get upset." She then picked up one of the toys and put it on the shelf. Immediately her children began to participate, and once they had gotten started, they were able to complete the task without further effort on her part.

SPIRITUALITY APPLICATION 3: OPENING TO LOVE

Since love is transcendent, it is beyond any description or conception. You can have a fuller experience of love if you move beyond ideas and open yourself to its presence. It is important to have practiced Centering Prayer and Practicing the Presence of Love before you try opening to a more transcendent experience of love. The first two techniques give you experiences you can use to begin the practice of Opening to Love.

While you need to start with some ideas or images of love, the fact that you will be opening means that you will be moving beyond your ideas. You'll be using your ideas to orient your mind in the proper direction, but then you have to let go of them.

As you practice Opening to Love, you may experience new or unusual ideas about love. You may see intense images, experience sounds, sense movements, or feel strong emotions. None of these have any real meaning. Enjoy them if they occur, but do not take them to be accurate messages about love. When you are truly open to transcendent love, the experience is not something your thinking mind will understand. Thoughts will occur, but they are not really relevant.

You may have some ideas or images about love that do not make much sense. This is a normal result. All the ideas, images, and feelings that occur during the experience are just side effects of what is, in essence, a completely spiritual experience.

So let the ideas, images, and feelings come, but use the skills you developed during the attending practices to disengage from them throughout the execution phase of the session. It is during the reflection phase of the exercise that you are to think about the ideas, images, and feelings you experienced. During the reflection phase your experiences are fresh in your memory and your thinking mind is active. Reflecting on the experiences you had during the openness will help you make sense of them and integrate them into your current understanding.

The exercise, Opening to Love, can induce a radically altered state of consciousness. That does not always happen, but you'll want to prepare for it in case it does. Make sure that you set aside enough time for the session so that you will be able to reorient yourself fully before you have to do anything else. This is not a technique that you should practice on your lunch hour at work, or just before driving somewhere. Set aside twenty to thirty minutes for the technique, but make sure you will have another thirty or so minutes afterward before you have to do anything active or stressful.

Do not use this exercise as the only spirituality exercise you practice. You should spend at least as much time in Centering

Prayer or the extended version of Practicing the Presence of Love as you do on Opening to Love. That means that you will practice Opening to Love once per week or less. Since you will practice it infrequently, you might schedule it for a weekend day, or some other day that is not too busy. Early morning or evening are good times to practice.

The Opening to Love technique is quite simple. You first remember your intention to experience complete love, transcendent love. Even if you don't know exactly what this is like, you must make it your intention anyway. Then concentrate on the experiences of love that you have had from Centering Prayer or Practicing the Presence of Love. The more strongly and clearly you are able to concentrate on those experiences, the better.

After concentrating on the experiences of love that you have had so far, simply do an opening technique. As you experience the vastness and space that come with opening, recall your experience of love from time to time.

BRIAN'S EXPERIENCE WITH OPENING TO LOVE

Brian, having had consistent success with Practicing the Presence of Love, is now beginning a session of Opening to Love. It is early on Sunday morning. He usually doesn't practice on Sunday, but he skipped Saturday's meditation session because he knew he would be less busy today.

Brian sits comfortably, closes his eyes, and remembers his intention to experience transcendent love and peace. He doesn't quite know what this means and wonders if he has done it correctly. He remembers what his teacher said: **"When you remember your** intention for this exercise, you won't have a complete idea of what you are trying to achieve. Simply be aware of your intention and then clarify it by concentrating on the experiences of peace and love you have had."

Brian identifies his thoughts about doing the technique "right" as judging himself, and disengages from them. He concentrates on the feeling of peace he has around and inside himself when he does the extended version of Practicing the Presence of Love. After a couple of minutes he senses the familiar presence of peace.

Brian then imagines that he is on a mountaintop. He imagines the experience of vastness as he sits above everything. He then concentrates on the presence of peace being with him there. He opens to the experience of vastness and imagines the peace filling it. Everywhere he looks there is peace. As the presence of peace grows in immensity and intensity, Brian feels that he is floating upward off the mountaintop, floating in an atmosphere of peace. His body absorbs the peace, expanding and contracting.

Soon Brian is aware *only* of peace. He is just vaguely aware of his body. There are no colors, images, thoughts, or emotions. He is simply aware of a presence that is completely at peace. He is not sure if *he* is that presence or if the presence is of another. It doesn't matter.

After a period of timelessness, Brian feels his awareness of his body returning. He struggles against it a bit, but remembers the advice of his teacher: **"The amount of time you can spend in the open state will be limited. Often your body starts getting restless after about twenty minutes. It is important to accept that without fighting it. The open state is quite enjoyable, but you can't force it. If you start to get restless and find yourself coming out of it, just accept that and allow your state of consciousness to gradually return to normal. The purpose of this is to move into a state in which you experience a connection with a spiritual presence. Then you are to use the other techniques to bring that presence more noticeably into your daily life."**

Brian reluctantly accepts the need to return from the experience. He feels his body sitting restfully and remembers the day and his surroundings. He reflects on the experience for a few minutes. He notices a desire to repeat this as often as possible, but he remembers a warning from his teacher. **"Be careful about becoming addicted to experiences. The purpose of this exercise is to give you a deeper experience of spiritual presence. But there is much more to spirituality than that. Bring that spiritual presence into your life and touch the world around you with it. That is why you are to practice one of the other spiritual applications in addition to this one."**

Brian takes several minutes to reorient fully to his body, the time, and his surroundings. He feels quite relaxed and happy. He notices that twenty-five minutes have gone by since he began the exercise. Since the morning is still young, he decides to take a walk before breakfast.

MARIA'S EXPERIENCE WITH OPENING TO LOVE

Maria is starting a session of Opening to Love. It is the third time she is trying the exercise. The first two times did not seem very satisfying. She did not get quiet inside and had lots of chaotic visual imagery. She and her teacher had discussed the problem. It turned out that Maria was expecting to have specific visual experiences. She expected to see white light, and she expected to see God as a person, probably wearing a robe. Maria struggled a bit before she could let go of these expectations. Her teacher was quite firm: **"When you open to love, you are to go beyond any limiting images or thoughts. You do not reject them, but you realize they do not show the complete reality of love. Love is infinite, whereas any image is quite finite. Your mind is too honest to let you get trapped by any stereotyped image. Concentrate on the idea you have experienced of patience and love. That is as close as your thinking mind can come to the**

infinite reality of love. Then open up to that and disengage from any other experiences as mere distractions."

Maria starts by focusing her intention to experience God's love in a transcendent way. She then relaxes and concentrates on the presence of love and patience that she is familiar with from Practicing the Presence of Love. After a few minutes, she experiences the feeling of being cradled by a motherly presence that is loving, patient, and understanding. Maria then uses the opening technique of feeling her body expand as she inhales and contract as she exhales.

As she uses that technique, Maria focuses from time to time on the patient and understanding presence around her. As she continues, she feels her awareness of her body change. She does not know quite where her body ends. Maria sees colors and shapes float past her. She starts to try to form the shapes into the image she thinks would be appropriate, the image of a person surrounded by white light. This seems difficult and the image does not form. Maria then hears the firm voice of her teacher: **"Do not try to make any particular image appear. Do not hold on to any image that arises. Simply concentrate on what you have experienced of patience and love, and continue to open to that. Any images that appear in this technique are just traps for your mind, so stay disengaged from them."**

Maria realizes that she is getting hooked, so she reminds herself of her intention and disengages from trying to make the image of a person and white light appear. She concentrates again on the experience of patience and love surrounding her and feels her body expand and contract. The colors and shapes return, but only briefly. Then she feels like she is becoming bigger and bigger and that inside her is nothing but patience and love. She continues to feel as if she is growing, spreading out to cover a huge area. All the while there is nothing but patience and love within her.

While she experiences this, images arise and disappear. Maria finds that if she focuses too much on an image, the feeling of love and patience loses some of its strength. So she simply notices the images and stays disengaged from them, concentrating instead on the idea of peace and love. After an unknown amount of time, Maria feels her normal body awareness returning. She allows herself to reorient slowly, remembering the day, the time, and her surroundings.

As she reflects on her experience, she realizes that she doesn't remember much except being in a state of peace and love that permeated her whole being. Still somewhat disoriented, she wiggles her fingers and toes and then flexes her arms and legs. She feels quite peaceful, patient, and loving. She takes her time getting up and then does some quiet activities around the house.

INSTRUCTIONS FOR SPIRITUALITY APPLICATION 3: OPENING TO LOVE

- Remember: Transcendent love is beyond our ability to describe. Spaciousness lets us go beyond our conceptual limitations to experience it more deeply.
- Begin by remembering your intention to open to the experience of love.
- Concentrate on the experience of love that you have had from either Centering Prayer, or Practicing the Presence of Love. The experiences from Practicing the Presence of Love are usually the clearest and easiest to concentrate upon.
- Next, do an opening technique. One of the following can be used:

  — Feel your body expanding and contracting as you breathe. Then imagine that love is filling the space that is expanding and contracting.

— Imagine being in a vast open space, like the top of a mountain. Imagine that love is surrounding you and fills the
vastness in every direction as far as you can perceive.

- Disengage from any images or thoughts and go back to concentrating on the idea of love filling the space. Keep opening
more and more.
- When you feel restless, or when your alarm signals you, then
stop and reflect on the experience.
- Reorient yourself slowly and thoroughly. Remember the
time, your surroundings, and stretch your body gently before
you get up.

TIPS FOR THE PRACTICE OF OPENING TO LOVE

- Feel as if the presence of love is going deeper and deeper
inside of you.
- Feel as if there is more and more space inside you and that it
is being filled with love.
- Variability in experience is common, both within the session
and between sessions.
- Your perception of the experience is not an accurate measure
of its benefit to your spirit.
- If you are experiencing distractions, it is important to simply
return to feeling the presence of love and then to reopen to
it. Your spirit can benefit even though your conscious mind is
caught up with distractions, as long as you are continuing to
disengage from the distractions and attempting to continue
the practice.
- When coming back, it is important to reorient to the normal
waking state thoroughly. If you feel disoriented, eating a light
snack can be helpful.

BRIAN'S AND MARIA'S RESULTS FROM OPENING TO LOVE PRACTICE

Brian has practiced Opening to Love every Sunday for the last three weeks. His experiences in the last two sessions were not as powerful as they were in the first session. He was a little disappointed, but his teacher had emphasized that Brian's perceptual changes, and the images that came to him, were not an accurate reflection of the benefit received from the technique.

Brian is noticing that he feels a connection with other people and the world that is quite peaceful. That feeling of peace is sometimes quite faint but is gradually growing stronger. He (correctly) perceives it as a welcoming of the presence of the other living things in the world and an understanding that the earth, air, sky, wind, clouds, sun, and rain are also alive and interconnected in some way. Brian is newly aware that he often acts and presents himself forcefully as he goes through his day, and realizes that this clashes with his sense of peaceful connectedness. He has realized that much of his forcefulness is unneeded, so he is trying to act more gently as he moves and speaks. He will be firm when he has to, but he knows that he does not have to be forceful all the time. As he deepens this experience of peaceful connection, his environment seems to respond, and people act more peacefully in his presence.

AFTER HER SESSIONS of Opening to Love, Maria retains a feeling of joy and peace for several hours. She wanted to practice more frequently, but her teacher advised her, **"Opening to Love can be very enjoyable, but you need to practice the other spirituality applications in order to keep from getting too spacey. When you're not grounded, you can't be of much use to anyone."** She practices three times in the next month. At the end of that month, she feels more serene. She can stay calm and peaceful, even if things are not going the way she wants. She has faith that things are really OK and that she doesn't need to be in control of them all the time. Her feeling of being in the presence of patience and love is more palpable, and she now has much more patience with others. This has a calming effect on the emotional atmosphere at home and at work.

REVIEW OF SPIRITUAL APPLICATIONS

The three spirituality applications we have described are the most important applications in the book. Inner peace requires more than health, prestige, and even good relationships with others; we all need a vivid, vital sense of connection with love. That comes from practicing the spirituality applications.

These three applications build on one another when practiced in sequence. Centering Prayer trains your mind to focus on something quite abstract, the idea of love, which in turn prepares it to concentrate on that idea and create a vivid experience of it in Practicing the Presence of Love. Once you have the experience of feeling love within and around you, the ability to direct your intention clearly enough in Opening to Love is yours.

The brief version of Practicing the Presence of Love is the most important of all the brief applications covered in this book. That technique will allow you to maintain a close connection with love, no matter what is going on around you. It is a superb antidote to the pressures of modern life. We recommend that you practice it daily, and preferably several times each day.

If you want to focus on the spiritual applications for a few weeks, then you can do so on a three-week cycle. Practice the extended attending, concentrating, and opening techniques for thirty minutes each during the three weeks to maintain your basic skills. Then use the rest of your extended sessions to practice the spiritual applications. A general recommendation is to practice Opening to Love once per week. Use the other extended sessions to practice Centering Prayer or Practicing the Presence of Love, whichever you prefer. Continue to do the brief practices for attending, concentrating, and opening as well as using a brief version of Practicing the Presence of Love several times per day.

11 overview: bringing basic meditation techniques into your daily life

YOU HAVE NOW learned a system of mental techniques to help you to find peace in your daily life, to develop your mental qualities, and to improve your health, enhance your performance, strengthen your relationships, and deepen your spirituality.

It is important to integrate these into your life in a balanced way. Obviously, you cannot practice all of the sixteen techniques in this book regularly, unless you are going to spend a lot more than ninety minutes per week meditating. Instead, you can rotate through the techniques systematically so that you can continue to improve in a balanced manner.

The basic techniques are used to develop the primary mental qualities. It is important to keep practicing them. You should spend thirty minutes per week practicing an extended basic meditation technique: either in attending, concentrating, or opening. You do not need to practice an extended centering technique because you will gain the benefits of that from doing concentrating. If you practice one basic technique per week, you will rotate through the three basic extended techniques in three weeks. That will be sufficient to keep honing your mental qualities.

You can spend the rest of your extended sessions practicing applications. The applications to spirituality are the most important. A deep spiritual connection is most closely associated with inner peace. Practice extended spirituality techniques for thirty minutes per week. You should alternate between Opening to Love and either Centering Prayer or Practicing the Presence of Love.

If you are spending the minimum amount of thirty minutes per week doing extended spiritual applications, that leaves at least thirty minutes per week for the other three areas—performance, health, and relationships. Thirty minutes per week is not enough time to work on all of them at once. However, you can spend one or more weeks working on one area, then move to another and still make progress. Of course, the more time you spend time practicing, the more you will be able to work on each of the applications.

As important as the extended techniques are, the brief techniques are even more important for integrating meditation into your daily life. With persistence you will be able to do ten to fifteen brief practice sessions easily during the course of the day. These brief sessions will give you a tremendous opportunity to maintain your skills and improve your application of them. To keep up your basic skills, you should practice the brief attending technique, "How Did I Get Here?," and the brief concentrating technique, "What Happened Then?," every day.

The most important of all the brief techniques is the short version of Practicing the Presence of Love. You should do that at least several times per day. Just after waking and just before sleeping are two good times for that. Short versions of Autonomic Relaxation or Inner Harmony can be used frequently to relieve stress. Even the brief centering technique of "Calm – Relaxed" can be used in this way. For times when you feel especially stressed, use the brief opening technique, "Instant Space," to get some relief.

If you are working on improving a relationship, then practice Building Positive Energy for a minute at a time, several times per day. If you are focusing on improving your performance at a specific task, then practice a short version of Directed Imagination several times per day.

By making a habit of practicing the brief techniques, you will be able to progress rapidly and have sufficient time to meet your other responsibilities.

Here is a summary of the techniques covered in this book. The material on the basic techniques is repeated from chapter 6. The suggested practice times we give are based on the minimum of ninety minutes per week doing extended sessions. If you spend more time doing the extended sessions, then you can do more than the minimums we've suggested. If you are not able to spend as much time as we suggest doing the extended sessions, then you can still benefit by practicing the brief techniques more frequently. For more ideas on creating a practice schedule, please see www.fullcapacityliving.com.

CENTERING: BASIC PRACTICE

Definition. Maintaining continuous awareness of a physical or mental object. The object you maintain awareness of is called your center.

Purpose. Develops mental steadiness and prepares you to do the more complex techniques of attending and concentrating.

Extended Technique. Focus on the sensations in your lower abdomen. If you get distracted, return your awareness to those sensations.

Brief Technique. Focus on a simple mental phrase such as "Calm – Relaxed" or "Calm – Alert" for thirty to sixty seconds.

Continued Practice. Not needed. You may use the brief technique for stress reduction during the day.

ATTENDING: BASIC PRACTICE

Definition. Identifying and disengaging from sensations, thoughts, and emotions.

Purpose. Develops mental flexibility and warmth.

Extended Technique. Focus on the sensations of air flowing in and out at the entrance of your nostrils or across your lips as you breathe. Identify and disengage from any distractions.

Brief Technique. Observe what sensations, thoughts, and feelings are going through your mind. Spend only ten to twenty seconds going over your experience for the preceding couple of minutes.

Continued Practice. Do the extended technique for a total of thirty minutes every three weeks. You are to rotate this with the extended techniques for concentrating and opening. Do the brief technique two or three times per day a couple of days per week.

CONCENTRATING: BASIC PRACTICE

Definition. Maintaining intense awareness of an object and perceiving it in complete detail without being distracted.

Purpose. Develops mental steadiness and clarity.

Extended Technique. Concentrate on the memory of a simple shape, a simple sound, or a simple movement.

Brief Technique. Concentrate for one to two minutes on the memory of an event that occurred earlier in the day.

Continued Practice. Do the extended technique for a total of thirty minutes every three weeks. This rotates with the extended techniques of attending and opening. Do the brief technique two or three times per day a couple of days per week.

OPENING: BASIC PRACTICE

Definition. Letting go of how the mind organizes perceptions so that a different perspective can arise.

Purpose. Develops mental spaciousness.

Extended Technique 1. Feel your chest and abdomen expand as you inhale and contract as you exhale. Imagine that your whole body is expanding and contracting as you breathe in and out.

Extended Technique 2. Imagine being in a wide-open place such as on a mountaintop. Imagine that everything is very far away, and feel your mind filling the vastness.

Brief Technique. Take a deep breath in and imagine it filling your whole body with lots of space. As you breathe out, imagine that the space is surrounding you and that everything is moving farther away.

Continued Practice. Do one of the extended techniques for a total of thirty minutes every three weeks. This rotates with the extended techniques of attending and concentrating. Do the brief technique as needed when you feel especially stressed.

AUTONOMIC RELAXATION: HEALTH APPLICATION 1

Uses Centering and Attending

Purpose. Relaxes several parts of the autonomic nervous system, enhancing the natural healing powers of the body.

Continued Practice. Practice going through the technique in two minutes and do this a couple of times per day for stress reduction.

INNER HARMONY: HEALTH APPLICATION 2

Uses Attending and Concentrating

Purpose. To create a more positive relationship between the mind and the body, which facilitates greater harmony among the body systems.

Continued Practice. Practice going through the technique in less and less time until you can feel results within a couple of minutes. Then use it a couple of times per day for stress reduction (unless you are using Autonomic Relaxation for that purpose).

HEALING LIGHT: HEALTH APPLICATION 3

Uses Attending, Concentrating, and Opening

Purpose. To create an altered state of consciousness directed by the intention for healing. This allows the mind to find indirect paths to a healthier state.

Continued Practice. Once per week if you are simply working on improving your general health. Up to twice per day if you are working on healing a medical condition.

HEIGHTENED FOCUS: PERFORMANCE APPLICATION 1

Uses Centering and Attending

Purpose. To enter a state in which you are calm, alert, and focused on everything that matters to performing your task while ignoring everything that is irrelevant.

Continued Practice. Use this while doing any task the performance of which you want to improve.

DIRECTED IMAGINATION: PERFORMANCE APPLICATION 2

Uses Attending and Concentrating

Purpose. To practice performing skills successfully in your imagination so that you are better able to do them in reality.

Continued Practice. Do the extended version until you can imagine the successful performance effortlessly. Then recall that briefly several times during the day. This is not needed unless you are working on improving at a specific task.

CLEARING BLOCKS: PERFORMANCE APPLICATION 3

Uses Attending, Concentrating, and Opening

Purpose. To help you overcome inner blocks to being successful. These blocks may come from prior events, or from pursuing goals that are not right for you.

Continued Practice. Use this if you are having difficulty with Directed Imagination, especially if Directed Imagination has stopped working.

BUILDING POSITIVE ENERGY: RELATIONSHIP APPLICATION 1

Uses Centering and Attending

Purpose. To restore your awareness of the positive aspects of any of your relationships.

Continued Practice. Do this for one to two minutes daily, even if your relationship is going well. Do the one-minute sessions several times a day for any relationship you are working on.

CLOSENESS DURING CONFLICT: RELATIONSHIP APPLICATION 2

Uses Attending and Concentrating

Purpose. To enable you to dialogue about a difficult issue with the other person without avoiding what you need to say or getting overwhelmed by emotions. This often gives you insight into what makes the issue difficult.

Continued Practice. Not needed unless there is an issue you need to work on.

SPACE WITHOUT DISTANCE: RELATIONSHIP APPLICATION 3

Uses Attending, Concentrating, and Opening

Purpose. To allow you to feel you have the space available for personal growth without feeling you have to be physically or emotionally distant from your partner.

Continued Practice. Use this if you feel trapped or closed in by a relationship. It is a good idea to use this once a month or so, even if things are going well.

CENTERING PRAYER: SPIRITUALITY APPLICATION 1

Uses Centering and Attending

Purpose. To place your mind in a state that is receptive to love and to disengage from distractions while doing so.

Continued Practice. You can use this in place of Practicing the Presence of Love for thirty minutes every other week.

PRACTICING THE PRESENCE OF LOVE: SPIRITUALITY APPLICATION 2

Uses Attending and Concentrating

Purpose. To create a vivid experience of love within and around you, and to train your mind to recall that experience quickly in response to a cue.

Continued Practice. Use the extended version of this for thirty minutes every other week. Do the brief version of this technique several times every day.

OPENING TO LOVE: SPIRITUALITY APPLICATION 3

Uses Attending, Concentrating, and Opening

Purpose. To allow your mind to experience love in a way that transcends conceptual limitations.

Continued Practice. Practice this thirty minutes every other week. You are to alternate this application with Practicing the Presence of Love.

BRIAN'S RESULTS AFTER ONE YEAR OF PRACTICE

Brian is sitting down to lunch with his sister, Karen. After exchanging the usual pleasantries, Brian reaches across the table and hands Karen a small, gift-wrapped box. Karen opens it and finds a heart-shaped pendant on a gold chain. She pauses in surprise and then looks at Brian, smiling. "Brian, it's beautiful. Thank you so much. But what for?"

"I wanted to thank you for your suggestion about a year ago. About meditation."

"You've really kept at it, haven't you?"

"Yes, and I'm glad I have. I'm doing better in a lot of ways."

"That's great, Brian. The family has noticed a lot of positive changes too. You are a lot less forceful, a lot less stressed, and yet still focused when you need to be."

"I feel better mentally and physically, and I'm a lot more peaceful inside."

"Are you going to keep meditating?"

"Of course. It took a while, but I am achieving the goals I set for myself, so why not keep going?"

"What are you going to work on now?"

"Well, I can't do everything at once."

"No, otherwise all that peace will disappear!"

"That's right. I'll continue the applications I've learned for bringing a greater sense of peace into my life, and I'll focus on increasing that at home. So that will be an ongoing project. While I'm doing that, I plan to work on getting into better physical shape. That's a good health goal, and I should reach it after a couple of months. My relationship goal is to improve my interactions with my coworkers, and my performance goal is to increase my efficiency at work. I'll probably alternate between those two for several months."

"Sounds like you have things planned out."

"Well, progress will take some time, but the time is going to pass anyway, so I might as well do something with it."

"I'm glad you're doing this, Brian."

"Me too. And thanks, again."

MARIA'S RESULTS AFTER ONE YEAR OF PRACTICE

Maria and her friend Susan are having a walk after dinner together. Susan says, "It was very nice of you to treat me to dinner, Maria. Thank you very much."

"Oh, my pleasure," Maria replied. "Besides, I owe you a lot for suggesting I take up meditation."

"It has made a difference, hasn't it?"

"Definitely. Instead of demands, I have *challenges*. As I deal with them, I feel like I am moving forward. I'm becoming a better person."

"What do you like best about what has happened?"

"Hmm, well, my spirituality has gotten deeper. Its gotten far more complex and more personal than I ever thought it could be."

"That sounds good."

"There is a whole feminine side to spirituality that I'm discovering, a quality I can relate to more easily."

"Beautiful. Anything else?" Susan queried.

"Well, I'm going to continue working on my spiritual life, but I also have some new goals."

"Such as?"

"I'd like to be at a healthier weight, and I think that would be a good health goal. But before I work on that, I'd like to start playing tennis. So I'll focus on using meditation to help me learn, and then my weight will probably adjust itself."

"Very good."

"And things are going well at home. After I learn tennis, I plan to focus on increasing the warmth and affection I have with Kevin. So that will be my new relationship goal."

"This all sounds great, Maria."

"You know, something? I really wish Kevin would do this too. He is quite supportive and appreciates the changes I've made, but he doesn't practice himself. Meditation would really help him."

"That's true, but the best way to get him interested is to keep up your own practice. As your life becomes more peaceful, he will get more interested."

"So I shouldn't try to talk him into it?"

"Exactly. But you can encourage him if he shows interest in what is clearly helping you."

"I get it. Like the way you told me about meditation a year ago."

"That's right."

"Thanks, Susan."

FINAL THOUGHTS

It has been our privilege to give you these instructions for personal and spiritual development. We'd like to leave you with some final reflections.

Working with your mind is like tending a garden. A garden needs frequent attention. You must keep up with the weeding and pruning. If you ignore the garden for too long, then the resulting mess can seem overwhelming. But even a couple of minutes of pulling weeds or tending the plants makes a difference when it is done regularly.

You must also be careful not to do too much. Too much water or fertilizer is just as damaging as not enough. If you are constantly digging up seeds to check on them, they will never sprout. So you must learn when to act and when to be patient.

Finally, the growth of a garden is always inevitably somewhat out of our control. Plants take a certain amount of time to develop, they cannot be rushed. Flowers will bloom on their own schedule, and fruits will ripen in their own time. You can influence these processes, but you cannot control them. So tend to your garden, your mind, with a gentle, patient touch. Listen to it to know where your effort needs to be applied. As you become aware of its rhythms, you'll more deeply sense what it needs.

Meditate frequently, but be gentle about it. Remember your intention at the start of the sessions, then let go of your intention and accept the experience. Weave the brief sessions into your day so that they become enjoyable habits. Then let the results come as they will. As you practice, you will become less concerned with goals, and the process itself will be increasingly enjoyable.

THE AUTHORS' OWN STORIES

LOBSANG: I was born in Lhasa, Tibet; the fourth in a family of nine children. When I was four, we fled the Chinese Communists, like thousands of other Tibetans, and escaped into India. I remember the sadness I felt at the misery and poverty of my fellow Tibetans as they streamed across the Indian border. Sometimes I would turn my head away to hide my grief and helplessness. I wanted to help them, and was fortunate to get accepted into a Catholic private school in India, where I received an excellent education.

When I was twenty years old, my father died. I decided to become a Buddhist monk, even though I had been schooled in a Western environment. I joined the Buddhist School of Dialectics started by His Holiness the Dalai Lama for young Tibetan monks. There I studied the ancient texts and learned to debate, pray, and meditate. I took advanced teachings and training from my root gurus, Kyabche Trichang Rinpoche, the Tutor to His Holiness the Dalai Lama, and from Khen Lati Rinpoche, the Abbot of Gaden Shartse Monastic College. Since I had both a Western education and knowledge of Buddhist scriptures, I worked as a deputy secretary and translator for His Holiness the Dalai Lama.

I enjoyed all this greatly, but I also wanted to understand how the Western mind worked, and felt that studying psychology in the West would be the way to do so. I felt deeply that I could be of better service to His Holiness and the Tibetan people by pursuing this interest. I discussed this with His Holiness, and he was very supportive of this. Since coming to the United States, I have completed my studies and am now a staff psychologist and Assistant Clinical Professor in Psychiatry at UCLA, as well as a clinical instructor at Harvard Medical School. I balance my work as a monk and my position in Western society with the sincere hope that I can make life meaningful for my people despite what has happened in Tibet.

JOSEPH: I was born in New York, the eldest of six children. I was raised Catholic, and as a child I became familiar with spiritual works by Christian mystics such as Teresa of Avila, John of the Cross, and Thomas Merton. I began practicing meditation when I studied martial arts in high school. I then went to college at CalTech. While pursuing my scientific training I also studied Zen and Christian contemplative prayer. I learned that I was interested in more than simply finding a system of meditation to study. I wanted to know how meditation influenced the mind-body system.

I continued to explore meditation through my years in college, medical school, and psychiatric training. By the time I became a psychiatrist, I had been practicing meditation for almost fifteen years. I had also studied psychology and mathematical theories of perception and consciousness. Through my studies and work with patients I came to believe that practical applications of spiritual ideas were vitally needed in modern society. At that time I attended a talk at a small bookstore near Los Angeles. It was a gray winter evening, and the speaker was Lobsang Rapgay.

When Lobsang and I met, we found we shared a strong desire to integrate Eastern and Western spiritual systems. We also shared the experience of meeting numerous people who wanted to change but did not know how. Many of these people had tried using meditation to make a positive change in their lives, but with disappointing results. Some of these people thought meditation was just for relaxing. Others had pleasant experiences during meditation but saw no positive changes in their personality. Some people were confused by the techniques, and their practice was ineffective. We even met a few people who were negatively affected by meditation. The techniques they were practicing were making their lives worse instead of better. We were disturbed; we knew that meditative systems had been designed to help people improve themselves. Furthermore we had each personally had powerful, personally transformative experiences with meditation. We knew that meditation had a lot more to offer than just relaxation and that it should lead to positive changes in one's personality as well as in all areas of life.

We were intensely motivated to explain meditation clearly enough so that Westerners could understand how to use it to create beneficial change in their daily lives.

THE PSYCHOLOGIST Carl Jung said that eventually the West would develop its own yoga, its own science of mental and spiritual transformation that was as precise and as effective as anything in the East. This book is a step toward that goal. For seven years we met frequently and practiced many types and variations of meditation techniques. As we practiced, we talked about the effect each technique had on our minds. We could sense and describe these effects because each of us had expertise in both meditation and psychology. We eventually learned enough to explain the principles underlying the techniques in purely Western terms.

As we worked together, we found that small differences in the techniques could cause great differences in our minds. We noticed patterns in the relationship between the techniques and their effects. We discovered that we could describe the mental effects of the techniques by referring to five mental qualities. We found that we could teach people how to develop these qualities, and how to use these qualities to improve their health, their performance, their relationships, and their spiritual lives.

Considering our different backgrounds, our work together has been remarkably smooth, and we have formed a deep and meaningful friendship, though much of it is unspoken. We seem to connect at a nonverbal, intuitive level. We pick up each other's thoughts and often finish each other's statements. Even when we discussed sensitive issues during the writing of this book, we could resolve our differences because of our mutual openness and respect for each other.

This mutual respect for each other's spiritual beliefs and training has enabled us to interact, not as a Westerner and an Easterner, but as two friends working as partners in a common endeavor. Lobsang was born into a Buddhist family in Tibet. Joseph was born into a Catholic family in New York. An amazing string of coincidences brought us together in Los Angeles. We hope that our collaboration can lead you to a deep experience of inner peace that will stay with you throughout your life.

About Wisdom Publications

Wisdom Publications, a nonprofit publisher, is dedicated to making available authentic works relating to Buddhism for the benefit of all. We publish books by ancient and modern masters in all traditions of Buddhism, translations of important texts, and original scholarship. Additionally, we offer books that explore East-West themes unfolding as traditional Buddhism encounters our modern culture in all its aspects. Our titles are published with the appreciation of Buddhism as a living philosophy, and with the special commitment to preserve and transmit important works from Buddhism's many traditions.

To learn more about Wisdom, or to browse books online, visit our website at www.wisdompubs.org.

You may request a copy of our catalog online or by writing to this address:

Wisdom Publications
199 Elm Street
Somerville, Massachusetts 02144 USA
Telephone: 617-776-7416
Fax: 617-776-7841
Email: info@wisdompubs.org
www.wisdompubs.org

THE WISDOM TRUST

As a nonprofit publisher, Wisdom is dedicated to the publication of Dharma books for the benefit of all sentient beings and dependent upon the kindness and generosity of sponsors in order to do so. If you would like to make a donation to Wisdom, you may do so through our website or our Somerville office. If you would like to help sponsor the publication of a book, please write or email us at the address above.

Thank you.

Wisdom is a nonprofit, charitable 501(c)(3) organization affiliated with the Foundation for the Preservation of the Mahayana Tradition (FPMT).

Additional Titles by Wisdom Publications

Ending the Pursuit of Happiness
A Zen Guide
Barry Magid
175 pages, ISBN 0-86171-553-5, $16.95

"This is an exceptional work, majestic in its scope and clarity. Barry Magid presents a mature vision and he does it with utmost care and intelligence. I really loved this book."—Mark Epstein, M.D., author of *Thoughts without a Thinker* and *Psychotherapy without the Self*

This surprising new book from Zen teacher, psychoanalyst, and critical favorite Barry Magid inspires us—in gentle and winking prose—to move on and make peace with the perfection of the way things actually are, including ourselves.

The Attention Revolution
Unlocking the Power of the Focused Mind
B. Alan Wallace
Foreword by Daniel Goleman
224 pages, ISBN 0-86171-276-5, $16.95

"This is the best kind of practical manual. I recommend this book to those of any spiritual tradition—or none—who wish to grow as human beings."—The Reverend Anthony Freeman, Editor of the *Journal of Consciousness Studies*

The Attention Revolution is an exciting, rewarding "expedition of the mind," tracing everything from the confusion at the bottom of the trail to the extraordinary clarity and power that come with making it to the top. Along the way, Alan also provides interludes and complementary practices for cultivating love, compassion, and clarity in our waking and dreaming lives.

Awakening Through Love
Unveiling Your Deepest Goodness
John Makransky
Foreword by Lama Surya Das
280 pages, ISBN 0-86171-537-3, $16.95

"*Awakening Through Love* is an uplifting and joyful reminder of our human potential. As a manual for practice, it wonderfully supports our shift from a contracted self-centeredness to the profound expansiveness of connection with others." —Sharon Salzberg, author of *Lovingkindness*

Mother Theresa. The Dalai Lama. Nelson Mandela. Gandhi. Some admire such figures from afar and think, How special they are; I could never be like that. But as John Makransky has learned, the power of real and enduring love lies within every one of us. *Awakening Through Love* is his guide to finding it.

Mindfulness Yoga
The Awakened Union of Breath, Body, and Mind
Frank Jude Boccio
Foreword by Georg Feuerstein
368 pages, ISBN 0-86171-335-4, $19.95

"It's about time somebody wrote this!"—Jon Kabat-Zinn, author of *Wherever You Go, There You Are*

Mindfulness Yoga emphasizes the spiritual side of yoga practice, an aspect often overlooked in a culture that tends to fixate solely on yoga's physical benefits. Unlike any other Buddhism-meets-yoga book, *Mindfulness Yoga* presents the two disciplines as a single practice that brings health to the body and liberates the mind and spirit, awakening compassion and fostering equanimity and joy. *Mindfulness Yoga* will appeal to the many people who have an interest in yoga, Buddhism, and meditation, but who may not have been able to find a teacher who could bring these practices together in a meaningful, practical way.